Lent with the Liturgy

REGINALD H. FULLER

Baldwin Professor
of Sacred Literature
Union Theological Seminary,
New York City

LONDON

S·P·C·K

1968

First published in 1969
by S.P.C.K.
Holy Trinity Church
Marylebone Road
London N.W.1

Made and printed in Great Britain by
The Talbot Press (S.P.C.K.),
Saffron Walden, Essex.

SBN 281 02319 0

LENT WITH THE LITURGY

IN MEMORY OF
MY FATHER
HORACE FULLER
1886-1964

CONTENTS

PREFACE   vii

ACKNOWLEDGEMENTS   viii

1   INTRODUCTION: LITURGY AND LENT   1

What is Liturgy?   1
The Church Year   10

2   WHAT IS LENT?   14

The Development of Passiontide and Holy Week   20

3   LENT AND PENITENCE (ASH WEDNESDAY)   23

Ash Wednesday: The Collect   27
Ash Wednesday: The Old Testament Lessons   31
Ash Wednesday: The Gospel   33

4   LENT AND LEARNING (LENT I-III)   35

Lent 1 (Invocabit): The Collect   35
(The Lenten Epistles: Lent 1-3)   36
Lent 1: The Epistle (2 Cor. 6. 1-10)   37
(The Gospels of Lent 1-3)   40
Lent 1: The Gospel (Matt. 4. 1-11)   41
Lent 2 (Reminiscere): The Collect   43
Lent 2: The Epistle (1 Thess. 4. 1-8)   45
Lent 2: The Gospel (Matt. 15. 21-28)   50
Lent 3 (Oculi): The Collect   53
Lent 3: The Epistle (Eph. 5. 1-14)   54
Lent 3: The Gospel (Luke 11. 14-28)   56

5   OASIS IN THE WILDERNESS: MID LENT   60

THE FOURTH SUNDAY IN LENT (LAETARE)   60
Lent 4: The Collect   62
Lent 4: The Epistle (Gal. 4. 21-31 and [5. 1a])   62
Lent 4: The Gospel (John 6. 1-14)   65

6 PASSIONTIDE   68

Passion Sunday (Judica): The Collect   69
Passion Sunday: The Epistle (Heb. 9. 11-15)   70
Passion Sunday: The Gospel (John 8. 46-59)   74
PALM SUNDAY   77
Palm Sunday: The Collect   78
Palm Sunday: The Epistle (Phil. 2. 5-11)   79
THE HOLY WEEK EPISTLES   83
Monday before Easter: Epistle (Isaiah 63. 1-19)   83
Tuesday before Easter: Epistle (Isaiah 50. 5-11)   87
Wednesday before Easter: Epistle (Hebrews 9. 16-28)   91
THE HOLY WEEK PASSIONS   93
Palm Sunday: St Matthew's Passion   97
Monday and Tuesday before Easter: St Mark's Passion   98
Wednesday and Thursday before Easter: St Luke's Passion   99
Good Friday: St John's Passion   100

7 THE TRIDUUM SACRUM   103

MAUNDY THURSDAY   104
GOOD FRIDAY   108
Good Friday: The Collects   109
Good Friday: Collect 1   109
Good Friday: Collects 2 and 3   110
Good Friday: The Third Collect   112
Good Friday: The Epistle (Heb. 10. 1-25)   113
EASTER EVEN: A PECULIARLY ANGLICAN INTERLUDE   113
Easter Even: The Collect   114
Easter Even: The Epistle (1 Pet. 3. 17-22)   115
The Gospel (Matt. 27. 57-66)   115
THE EASTER VIGIL   115
THE EASTER VIGIL SERVICE AND PASCHAL EUCHARIST   117

APPENDIX   123

THE PRAYER BOOK EASTER DAY   123

PREFACE

Ever since I first published *What is Liturgical Preaching?*
(London, 1957), I have been repeatedly asked whether I might
produce a whole series of *Predigtmeditationen* for the whole
Church Year, similar to the sample ones which were included
in that book. A partial opportunity to fulfil this request came when
in 1962 I was invited by a group of Lutheran Clergy in the
Chicago area to speak to them on Ash Wednesday on the subject
of "Lent with the Liturgy".

It is from these addresses that the present work has grown.
Most of its allusions to the American Lutheran Liturgy have been
shorn from the text, though a few have been retained—designedly,
because Anglicans (for whom in the main the present work is
intended) are often a little inclined in a somewhat insular way to
imagine that they alone of the Churches which passed through the
Reformation have retained substantial treasures from pre-
Reformation days. (Only the other day I saw an egregious
instance of this, in which it was suggested that the reckoning of
Sundays after Trinity instead of after Pentecost was an Anglican
peculiarity *vis-à-vis* Rome, when, as a matter of fact, the
Lutherans follow this reckoning too).

In these days, when the Calendar and Lectionary are facing the
prospect of total overhaul, it may seem a little rash to offer a
work based on the unreformed arrangements of both. But it will
be some years before the reforms at present being mooted become
universal, and it may even be that some of the points made in
this work will contribute towards such reform—particularly the
stress on the importance of the *Transitus* concept of the Christian
paschal celebration.

REGINALD H. FULLER

Advent 2, 1967.

ACKNOWLEDGEMENTS

Quotations from the *Revised Standard Version of the Bible,* copyrighted 1946 and 1952 by the Division of Christian Education of the National Council of Churches of Christ in the United States of America, are used by permission.

The Book of Common Prayer 1662 is Crown copyright; extracts used herein are by permission.

Thanks are due to the following for permission to quote from copyright sources:

J. M. Dent & Sons Ltd. (Everyman Library): *Sermons on Christian Doctrine,* by W. F. Robertson

S.C.M. Press Ltd and The Macmillan Company: *Letters and Papers from Prison* and *The Cost of Discipleship,* by Dietrich Bonhoeffer.

S.C.M. Press and Harper & Row, Publishers: *Life Together,* by Dietrich Bonhoeffer.

1

INTRODUCTION
LITURGY AND LENT

What is Liturgy?

The Churches of the Anglican Communion are often referred to as "liturgical Churches", a characteristic which we share with the Orthodox, Roman Catholic, and Lutheran Communions. By this is commonly meant that our services of worship, particularly those on a Sunday morning, are fixed. The service is not an *ad hoc* compilation of the pastor or priest, but read out of a book—the Book of Common Prayer. Although we have been a liturgical Church ever since the Reformation, it cannot be said that we have always valued the liturgy or understood it aright. To many people, especially in the pews, the liturgy is often just incidental to the sermon. Morning Prayer is often thought of as "the pre-liminaries", just as in Lutheranism the liturgy is often regarded as the introduction and conclusion to the sermon, or at the very most providing the "pericopes" or scriptural passages to be expounded in the sermon. Nor can it be claimed that our Roman Catholic brethren have been better off than ourselves. For them the liturgy has often been a courtly pageant to a degree that ours has never been. Their real religion and devotion, real prayer, have until the recent reforms been carried on very often in spite of rather than by means of the liturgy. If for us it has often provided the framework for the sermon, for them it has provided the framework for individual devotion.

If it is from such backgrounds that we come, we shall be surprised at our topic: Lent and the Liturgy. For Lent to us has

1

often seemed to provide an opportunity for increased individual religious devotion. The liturgy seems to have no positive, intrinsic value of its own. However, we are living in an age which has witnessed the liturgical movement. This movement is not to be thought of as an attempt merely to step up the pageantry of our services. It is not just an attempt to go back, for instance, to some earlier period—baroque, medieval, or patristic.[1] The liturgical movement is not just a craze to make our services more "high church". Rather it seeks to understand liturgy as an integral and indispensible part of the gospel itself. A staggering claim, that! Just the sort of thing you might expect from an antiquarian scholar with an ecclesiastical sort of mind. How can you claim that the forms of service in the Book of Common Prayer are "essential" to Christianity? After all, what of those denominations and confessions which have no liturgy as we have? At the most, all we could claim is that liturgy is of the *bene esse*, the well-being of the Church, certainly not of its *esse*, its very being. Yet this is what the liturgical movement is trying to put across. How can such things be?

It all depends really on what we mean by liturgy. If what we mean by it is simply fixed forms of prayer read out of a book, then obviously we cannot claim that such forms are of the *esse* of the Church. For that would not only unchurch the Free Churches of today, it would also unchurch the Church of the New Testament and of the first 150 years of Christian history. For there were no fixed forms of service in the Church anywhere, so far as we know, until somewhere about 200 A.D.[2]

Previously the sort of situation envisaged in the early Church Order known as the *Didache* or *Teaching of the Twelve Apostles* obtained: "Permit the prophets to offer thanksgiving (eucharist) as much as they desire" (*Did.* X, 7). Clearly, when we claim that the liturgy is essential to Christianity, we cannot mean simply that our form of worship should be fixed, and read out of a book.

What then is liturgy? If it simply means worship, then probably most of us (unless we are the sort of Christians who prefer to

[1] I.e. of the age of the Church Fathers (*c.* A.D. 100-800).

[2] The earliest known written liturgy is that of Hippolytus (date *c.* A.D. 200) and even that was something of a novelty.

2

spend Sunday on the golf course and "live a decent life from Monday to Saturday") would agree that worship is somehow integral and essential to Christianity. But liturgy means (at any rate in Christian history and in the liturgical movement) something a little more precise than that.

The word liturgy is a Greek word, compounded from two other words, *laos* meaning "people" and *ergon* meaning "work". It thus meant originally any work performed in the public service (in the political community of the ancient Greek city state). A wealthy man who financed the drama competitions in which the great plays of the Greek dramatists, such as Aeschylus, Sophocles, and Euripides, were first produced, was performing a "liturgy". So was a wealthy man who furnished a ship for the city state in time of war. Such was the word's original use.

In Greek the word "liturgy" underwent two developments. First, it became generalized to mean any kind of service, whether public or not. A slave performing his duties to his master was said to be doing his "liturgy". Secondly, and perhaps arising out of the purely general, private use, it came to be applied to a service done to a god, especially in the cultus.

It is not quite clear, but on the whole it is probable, that it was this last usage which led the Greek translators of the Old Testament to use the Greek word "liturgy" for the ritual acts performed by the Old Testament priests in the Temple, and especially for the offering of sacrifices.

The New Testament reflects both the secular and the cultic uses of the word "liturgy". Sometimes it occurs in exactly the Old Testament cultic sense. One case in point is the reference to Zechariah, the father of John the Baptist. "And when his time of service [Greek, "liturgy"] was ended, he went to his home" (Luke 1. 23). Similarly, the word "liturgy", whether as a noun or as a verb ("to perform the liturgy") occurs not infrequently in the discussion of the Old Testament sacrifices and priesthood in the Epistle to the Hebrews. Clearly, none of these occurrences represents a distinctively Christian usage, and none of them serves to substantiate our claim that liturgy is essential to Christianity.

Again, there are passages which reflect the ordinary, weakened, non-technical sense of "service". St Paul speaks of his

3

churches' collection for the saints at Jerusalem as their performance of a "liturgy" (Rom. 15. 27 [verb]; 2 Cor. 9. 12), and of the Philippians' dispatch of a gift to himself while he was in prison as a "liturgy" (RSV: "service") (Phil. 2. 30; cf. 2. 25). It would be wrong to look for any profound theological meaning behind the use of 'liturgy" in these passages, and none of them can be used to substantiate our claims that liturgy is essential to Christianity.

Three further passages remain to be discussed. One of them is Acts 13. 2, "While they were worshipping [literally: 'performing liturgy to'] the Lord . . .". At first sight it looks as though this passage might justify the conclusion that "liturgy" is used here with some profound theological sense and treated as a central activity of the Christian community at Antioch. But on closer inspection it appears to reflect no more than the ordinary cultic sense of the word "liturgy" which had established itself in ordinary Greek usage even before the Septuagint (Greek Bible) took up the use of the word (see above).

The second passage is Phil. 2. 17 which RSV translates: "Even if I am to be poured as a libation upon *the sacrificial offering* [literally: sacrifice and liturgy] of your faith . . .". Here St Paul speaks of his whole ministry as a "liturgy". It is a life of sacrificial service which he expects very soon to culminate in martyrdom. Can we press this passage to imply a profound theological interpretation of the Christian ministry as a liturgical one in the technical sense of the word? It is extremely doubtful. Probably the use of cultic language here is simply metaphorical, like Rom. 15. 6 and the similar language in Rom. 12. 1 ("I appeal to you, therefore, brethren, by the mercies of God, to present your bodies as a living sacrifice, holy and acceptable to God, which is your spiritual worship" [the Greek here is *latreia,* a word closely akin in meaning to *leitourgia*]).

The third passage, (Heb. 8. 6), however, is very different. Here the word "liturgy" is applied to the saving work of Christ himself: "Christ has obtained a ministry [liturgy] which is as much more excellent than the old". This verse occurs in the central part of the Epistle to the Hebrews, which sets up a contrast between the Old Testament priesthood and sacrifice and the

4

saving work of Christ. Christ, in his atoning death, his ascension and his heavenly intercession at once fulfills and supersedes the "liturgy" of the old covenant. Here the word "liturgy" is clearly applied to the very heart and core of the gospel, the saving work of Christ himself. But while this put the word "liturgy" right in the centre, and seems to justify our claim that liturgy is essential to Christianity, it appears to speak of that essential liturgy as Christ's work, and his alone, not as a liturgy performed by the Church. To speak of the Church's liturgy in anything beyond a general cultic sense as in Acts 13. 2 or in the spiritualized ethical sense of Phil. 2. 17 or Rom. 12. 1 seems to be ruled out precisely by Heb. 8. 6. Our claim that liturgy as an action of the Church is essential to Christianity seems to fall to the ground.[3]

But before we jump to that conclusion let us probe a little more deeply into the New Testament evidence. It may be that when the liturgical movement uses the word "liturgy" today it is speaking of something that is present in the New Testament, which is recognized there as something essential to the life of the Church, but which is never actually called by the name "liturgy".

Now it is true that the New Testament asserts that the saving act of God in Christ (and no one can doubt that *this* is the very centre and core of Christianity, the very substance of gospel) happened *once for all*:

"Christ died for our sins in accordance with the scriptures" (I Cor. 15. 3).

"The death he died he died to sin, *once for all*" (Rom. 6. 10).

"He has appeared *once for all* at the end of the age to put away sin by the sacrifice of himself" (Heb. 9. 26).

"Christ, having been offered *once* to bear the sins of many . . ." (Heb. 9. 28).

"For Christ also died for sins *once for all*" (1 Pet. 3. 18).[4]

It is this "once for all" event that is alone described as "liturgy" in the strict sense by the New Testament (Heb. 8. 6).

[3] It is the weakness of Alfred R. Shands, *The Liturgical Movement and the Local Church* (London, 1959), pp. 18-20, that he traces the Christian use of the word "liturgy" in an essential sense to the passages discussed above.

[4] All italics mine.

5

Yet the New Testament asserts just as strongly that this once-for-all event, which happened decisively in the past, is nevertheless something that does not belong merely to the past, to history. For Christ is risen from the dead. That means, among other things, he has been taken by God out of past history and made ever available to us as our contemporary. His past history (without ever being repeated) can henceforth become ever and again a present reality for us who believe. How does this happen?

First of all in the preaching of the saving act itself. Then the saving act becomes present to faith and the believer participates in it. Preaching is not just reporting a past event, but making what happened in the past a present reality to those who accept the message. The power of God to salvation, which was present in the cross on the first Good Friday is equally present in the preaching of the Word.

"The word [i.e. preaching] of the cross is folly to those who are perishing, but to us who are being saved it is the power of God" (1 Cor. 1. 18). It is the "message of reconciliation" (2 Cor. 5. 19)—not merely in the sense that it reports about reconciliation accomplished in the past, but through the apostles' preaching and the acceptance of that preaching in faith the reconciliation accomplished once for all on the cross is made a present reality in which the Christian community partakes.

Similarly, the preaching is the "message of this salvation" (Acts 13. 26). Often, too, in his letters the apostle Paul attributes to the preaching of the word the same effect as that of the cross itself. In preaching, the once-for-all event of the cross is not merely reported as a present event: without being repeated it becomes a present reality.

The effect which is here ascribed to the preaching of the word is similarly ascribed to the two sacraments of baptism and the Lord's Supper. In baptism, the Cross of Christ, without being repeated, becomes a present reality in which the baptized participates:

"All of us who have been baptized into Christ Jesus were baptized into his death" (Rom. 6. 3). In baptism we were "crucified with him" (Rom. 6. 6), and "died with Christ" (v. 8). At every celebration of the Lord's Supper, in the actual rite, not only

6

in the accompanying preaching, the Lord's death is "proclaimed" (1 Cor. 11. 26). Here "proclaimed" must mean exactly what it means in preaching the gospel: in the rite of the Lord's Supper, the saving event of the Lord's death is not merely announced as an occurrence of the past, nor is it repeated, of course, but it "becomes *here and now operative by its effects*".[5]

In these words Paul is giving in his own words what the tradition of the Lord's words at the Last Supper had given him: "Do this as a *memorial of me* (1 Cor. 11. 24 NEB; cf. Luke 22. 19 in the longer text, given in the margin of RSV and NEB). When the Jews made a "memorial" before God, as they did in the Passover, they did not merely remember what had happened in the past but, by their reciting it in adoration and thanksgiving before God, God made it a present reality, "operative by its effects". For the Jew believed that when he celebrated the passover he was actually there, coming out of Egypt with his forefathers.

The result of this proclamation, this memorial done in the rite, is that the congregation partakes in the saving event: "The cup of blessing which we bless, is it not a participation in the blood of Christ [i.e. in the saving event of his sacrificial death]? The bread which we break, is it not a participation in the body of Christ [i.e. himself, his person, actually present to his people]"? (1. Cor. 10. 16).

The preaching of the word, the rite of baptism and the celebration of the Lord's Supper, are thus all of them media by which the once-for-all saving event is made present by the act of God in and through the obedient acts of man.

For the preaching of the word, the rite of baptism, and the celebration of the Lord's Supper are all of them human acts, done by men. But they are also done in obedience to the Lord's commands as recorded in the New Testament:

"Go into all the world and preach the gospel to the whole creation" (Ps-Mark 16. 15; cf. Matt. 28. 19a).

"Baptizing them in the name of the Father and of the Son and of the Holy Spirit" (Matt. 28. 19b).

[5] G. Dix, *The Shape of the Liturgy* (London, 1945), p. 161 (Author's italics).

"Do this as a memorial of me" (1 Cor. 11. 24, 25 NEB; cf. Luke 22. 19f., long text).

Now it is these three actions—preaching, baptism, and the Lord's Supper—which comprise what we call "liturgy" in Christian usage. The New Testament, it is true, avoids calling these three actions by the name "liturgy" (the only possible exception would be Acts 13. 2, but the allusion to fasting accompanying the liturgy there does not make it likely that they were celebrating the Lord's Supper). They are the means through which God makes present the supreme and sole liturgy of the Christian dispensation, the saving act of God in Christ. So in this essential though derivative way we may use the word "liturgy" to apply to baptism, the Lord's Supper, and the proclamation of the word which accompany them. We need not be too worried that the word "liturgy" itself is not used in the New Testament in this essential though derivative way. After all, the word "sacrament" occurs nowhere in the New Testament, and yet most of us (except the Baptists!) use it without compunction. For in each case the thing is there, even if the word is absent. To refuse to use the word because it is not found in the Bible is sheer biblicism, which Anglicans have sensibly rejected.

We may, then, define liturgy in the New Testament and Christian sense, as primarily the saving work of God in Christ, wrought once for all on the cross, and yet ever present and available in its effects until the end of time. In a secondary and derivative sense it refers to those human activities performed in the Church—preaching, baptizing, and celebrating the Lord's Supper—in and through which God by his gracious act and in accordance with his promise makes present the primary "liturgy", the saving work of Christ.

It will be seen that liturgy in this second and derivative sense has the following characteristics:

1. It is action. It does not necessarily require a set form of words to accompany it. The gospel is preached, people are immersed in water, bread and wine are taken, a thanksgiving or blessing is said over them, the bread is broken, the bread and wine are given, taken, and consumed.

2. It is obedient action. It is not a cultic action invented by men, even though it has a cultic character.

3. It is action to which promises from God in Christ as witnessed by the apostolic Church and preserved by Scripture are annexed. It is therefore not magic. The effects of the action are brought about not by the performance of the cultic rites *in themselves*, but by the promise of God annexed to their obedient performance. That promise is accepted by the Church in faith.

4. Holy Scripture does not prescribe more than the bare outline of what is to be done in baptism and the Lord's Supper. So long as the essential basic acts are performed it is left to the Church to implement its obedience, e.g. the precise manner in which the actions are performed or the exact wording of the thanksgiving in the Lord's Supper.

Points 1, 2, and 3 substantiate our initial claim that liturgy is essential and integral to Christianity. It is not only that the Lord has commanded these things to be done in his Church: they are appointed means by which the once-for-all salvation is made ever present. In speaking of the necessity of liturgy, we were really saying what Article XIX says when it speaks of the necessity of word and sacraments to the being of the Church:

> The visible Church of Christ is a congregation of faithful men, in which the pure Word of God is preached, and the Sacraments be duly ministered according to Christ's ordinance in all those things that of necessity are requisite to the same.

In Point 4 (above) we encounter a third, tertiary sense of the word "liturgy". In its obedient carrying out of the scriptural commands, "do this", the Church has been free to select or devise prayers, readings, or formulas of its own. Already from the start, and from the very nature of the case, this was so with regard to the giving of thanks in the Lord's Supper. Gradually thereafter other prayers came into use, e.g. intercessions, devotional preparations, and thanksgiving for the reception of sacraments, lectionaries, and also subsidiary actions, or ways of doing the prescribed actions. We often refer to those set forms of words and actions, of rite and ceremony, when we speak of "liturgy". But this is only the third, derivative, tertiary sense of the word. No one can claim that *in this sense* liturgy is *essential* to Christianity or to the being of the Church. This is recognized again by the Thirty-nine Articles:

> It is not necessary that Traditions and Ceremonies be in all places one, and utterly alike; for at all times they have been divers, and many be changed according to the diversities of countries, times, and men's manners, so that nothing be ordained against God's Word (Art. XXXIV).

These non-essential rites and ceremonies are the outworks of liturgy proper. They underline and embellish it—but they may also obscure, pervert, or even suppress the bare essential acts which comprise our obedience. But there is often a great treasury of devotion in these tertiary parts of the liturgy. It is with these parts that we shall be concerned in our treatment of Lent and the Liturgy.

The Church Year

The major and controlling aspect of these outworks of the liturgy as we have them in Western Christendom—they are much more developed in the West than in the East—is the Church (or Christian) Year.[6]

The purpose of this yearly cycle is not only to provide consecutive series of themes for the preacher (though, of course, it does that). It is rather to accentuate in turn the various facets of the one saving event in which we participate in the liturgy. Of course, it is true that in every celebration of the liturgy we participate in the whole saving event (a truth which the Eastern church tends to emphasize more than we do). But for us finite men in time it is indeed helpful to concentrate upon one aspect of the total complex of the saving event. The "propers", i.e. the

[6] It is significant that in the East the liturgical colour—i.e. the colour of the vestments etc.—is invariably white, whereas in the West we use several different colours. The East concentrates throughout the year on the redemptive event in its unitary aspect. The West breaks it down into its component parts, as the colours of the rainbow are the constituent parts of light.

10

variable portions of the liturgy—the collects, Old Testament lessons and/or epistles, and gospels—all serve to accentuate some part of the total act of redemption in which we participate at any given season.

In this context we might indeed speak of the Christian "mystery", a concept which has played a central role in the theology of the Roman Catholic liturgical movement, especially in the thought of Dom Odo Casel of Maria Laach. Such language perhaps does not come readily to the evangelical Christian, but it is after all a biblical concept (e.g. Eph. 3. 9-11), and a Prayer Book one ("By the mystery of thy holy Incarnation . . ."). The "mystery" is the act of divine redemption revealed in Jesus Christ and made present for our participation in the "holy mysteries", the liturgy. Indeed, we may say that the liturgy of every Sunday and Holy Day has been distilled out of the one supreme liturgy of Easter, the paschal liturgy. This statement is in fact literally and historically true. For in the primitive church the paschal liturgy was a "commemoration" not only of the resurrection of the first Easter Day, but of the total act of God in Christ for our redemption—of Christ's coming into the world, his life, death, resurrection, and ascension, his reigning at the right hand of God, the coming of the Holy Spirit in the life of the Church, and, by anticipation, of his coming again. It was also a "commemoration" —in the biblical sense of that word (see above). And each Sunday was a "little Easter Day", a weekly celebration of the redemption.

In course of time the Church year was developed by the breaking up of the old Christian paschal feast into its constituent parts. Thus eventually we got Advent, Christmas, Epiphany, Lent, Palm Sunday, Holy Week, Maundy Thursday, Good Friday, Holy Saturday (Easter Even), Easter Day, the Great Forty Days, Ascension Day, the Ten Days Waiting, and finally Pentecost (Whitsunday). With this development there also came a loss of the older biblical idea of "commemoration". No longer did Christians understand themselves as actually sharing in or reliving the events which each feast commemorated. Rather, as we naturally do, they thought of themselves as simply "re-membering" these events, meditating on them as events that had happened way back in the past, mentally recalling them. Now we cannot put the clock back and return to the original paschal feast as the single, unitary feast of our redemption. We have grown used to the Church year, and it is filled with over a thousand years of Christian devotion and experience. But we do need to make an effort to recover the older, biblical idea of commemoration. Indeed, such a recovery is one of the chief aims of the liturgical movement.

First we must try to recover the idea that in the liturgy we are in a very real sense reliving the events that took place long ago. We are participating in them as saving "mysteries", as acts of God through which we are now being saved, not just as events through which we were in the past saved once and for all.

Secondly, we must try to realize that the single, separate events which we commemorate at each separate feast of the Church year are really parts of a single indivisible whole. When, for instance, we commemorate the birth of our Lord at Christmas we are commemorating it not as a separate event by itself, but as part of a single, total complex, the great act of our redemption which is God's whole act in Christ.

It is the loss of this sense of the totality of every separate feast that accounts for the widespread feeling among Protestants that somehow or other the Lord's Supper would be inappropriate at Christmas or on Easter Day. Why, it is sometimes asked, should we commemorate the death of Christ on a day when we are celebrating his birth, or when we are celebrating the resurrection? The answer of course is that we should not isolate his birth or resurrection from the other "mysteries" of our redemption. For each separate "mystery" is a part of the total mystery. It is the total mystery which is set forth and relived in every eucharistic celebration, despite the fact that with our developed Church year we stress particularly one aspect of the mystery. Regarded in this light, Christmas becomes truly the "Christ-Mass"—the celebration of our total redemption in Christ, and the proper celebration of Christmas is not a service of carols and readings (though this is an additional and helpful auxiliary and preparatory

7 The popular service of nine lessons and carols is a modern revival of the old vigil service which was preparatory to the Christmas eucharist. It is out of place *after* the Christmas eucharist.

devotion to the Christmas celebration), but the Mass, traditionally celebrated at midnight.[7]

Equally mistaken is the notion that the proper commemoration of Easter is a sunrise service in the romantic setting of the open air, a common custom in American Protestantism. This, too may be valuable as subsidiary devotion. But the real celebration of Easter is, again, the Lord's Supper. Once more we may not say that it is inappropriate to commemorate the death of Christ on the day when we are celebrating his resurrection. For this again would be to isolate one aspect of the total mystery. On Easter Day we now, with the developed Church year, *accentuate* the resurrection, but we must not isolate it from the total mystery of our redemption.

2

WHAT IS LENT?

If what we have said in the foregoing section is true of all the feasts of the Church year—namely, that they have been split off from the original single feast of our redemption at the Christian paschal feast—this is particularly true of Lent. In a very real sense the primitive paschal feast has been spread over the whole period from pre-Lent to Pentecost.

Let us consider how the earliest Christians observed their paschal feast. Like the Jews, they prepared for their passover by a preliminary fast. For the Jews the purpose of fasting was manifold. Primarily it was (as the New Testament shows: Luke 2. 37; Acts 13. 2, 14. 23) a reinforcement of prayer. Not only did fasting have the psychological effect of adding earnestness of concentration to prayer, but it was believed somehow to strengthen the urgency of the prayer, make it more prevalent in God's sight. Again, fasting was often undertaken as an act of penitence for one's own sins and even as an act of reparation for the sins of others. Sometimes it was an expression of mourning for the dead. Probably, however, the main reason for the fast before the passover was to enhance the sense of participation in the *transition* from the bondage of Egypt into the promised land. It was to help the worshippers feel that they were actually reliving that transition, actually experiencing the turn from sorrow into joy.

We may conjecture that this too was the basic reason for the fast before the Christian paschal feast. For the essential experience of the Christian paschal feast was likewise one of transition: from the bondage of sin to the glorious liberty of the children

14

of God, from sin unto righteousness, from darkness to light, from death to life and from sorrow to joy. This idea of transition is absolutely essential to the liturgical experience of Lent and Eastertide. It has its roots deep in the older Jewish tradition and is epitomized in the central mystery of our redemption, the death and resurrection of Christ.

Other motives, it is true, played a part in the pre-paschal Christian fast. Already in the Gospels there is some suggestion that it was an act of mourning. It occurred on the day that the bridegroom was taken away (Mark 2. 20, "in that day"). Sometimes there is the suggestion of reparation for the Jews' sin in crucifying the Messiah. This is particularly suggested by the timing of the fast. For in some areas at least (those which maintained the keeping of the Christian passover on 14th-15th Nisan, the exact day of the Jewish passover, on whatever day of the week it fell[1]), the fast coincided with the hours when the Jews were eating their passover. The Christians waited until the Jewish feast was over (i.e., midnight or after) before they broke off their fast and began their feast. There is also some suggestion that they delayed the feast until midnight in case the second coming should occur, when they would eat and drink with the Messiah in his kingdom. Failing that, they did the next best thing, celebrating the anticipation of his coming in the Lord's Supper.

We may perhaps imagine the Christians in apostolic times as keeping fast through the 14th Nisan with the Jews, then prolonging this fast from the beginning of the 15th Nisan (at sundown) until dawn or cockcrow. Then they proceeded to the Christian passover feast. The Exodus story of the Old Testament

[1] This was the custom in Asia Minor. Other places, e.g. Rome, kept the Christian passover always on the nearest Saturday-Sunday. Both parties claimed apostolic tradition for their custom. In the end the Church settled in favour of Saturday-Sunday. This loosened somewhat the Jewish connections of the Christian feast, but the variable date of Easter is still a witness to that connection. Perhaps the one cogent reason against the fixing of Easter (which now even Rome is prepared to accept) is that it will obscure the Jewish origin and associations of the feast. No doubt it is too much to hope that the Jewish community will fix the passover to coincide with a fixed Christian Easter!

would be read (Exod. 12)[2] and the story of the Lord's passion and resurrection.[3]

Following these readings would come the Lord's Supper, embracing at this time both with the "agape" (love feast) and the eucharistic proper.

The details are not altogether clear, and some of the above suggestions are mere guess-work. But the main outline is probably not far from what actually happened in the Christian Church in New Testament times. It is in this primitive paschal celebration that the earliest roots of our present Lent and Easter lie.

Another root of our modern Lent and Easter is the custom of administering baptism at Easter. How early this began we do not know. It is certain that it was well established in the second century. Indeed the New Testament itself already connects baptism with the death and resurrection of Christ:

> Do you not know that all of us who have been baptized into Christ Jesus were baptized into his death? We were buried therefore with him by baptism into death, so that as Christ was raised from the dead by the glory of the Father, we too might walk in the newness of life (Rom. 6. 3f.).

and in the sub-apostolic writing, 1 Peter:

> By his great mercy we have been born anew [note the baptismal language!] to a living hope through the resurrection of Jesus Christ from the dead (1 Pet. 1. 3).

The combination of paschal and resurrection language with baptismal themes throughout this epistle has suggested to some scholars that it was actually composed as a baptismal homily for use at Easter baptisms, either late in the first century or early in

[2] We know that this lesson was used in such widely differing Churches as Rome and Sardis in Asia at the end of the second century. The fact that they agree over this while disagreeing over the date of the paschal feast, together with the fact that the Jews used the same lesson, strongly suggests that its use goes back to the earliest Christian times and that it was taken over from Judaism. Paul's words in 1 Cor. 5. 7f., "Christ our paschal lamb, has been sacrificed. Let us, therefore, celebrate the festival", almost look like an early Christian homily on this lesson!

[3] Modern New Testament scholars hold that the passion stories took shape in liturgical use prior to their writing down in our Gospels.

the second. It may not, therefore, be altogether fanciful to suggest that already in apostolic and sub-apostolic times the administration of baptism was connected with Easter. Whether this is so or not, the association of Easter and baptism has theological significance in the New Testament, as the above quotations show.

We know definitely that by the second century the lessons read at the Christian passover celebration and the bishop's homily[4] were followed by the baptism of new converts to the Christian faith (for at that time, as in all missionary situations, adult baptism was the normal practice). The newly baptized then participated in the Lord's Supper for the first time, proceeding at once to enjoy their new privileges.

In the middle of the second century, the candidates had to undergo a period of fasting in preparation for the baptism. The earliest mention of this is in Justin Martyr, writing at Rome about A.D. 150. A little later Hippolytus, also at Rome (date *c.* A.D. 200), clearly implies a longer period of preparation for baptism than a two day fast. This time was filled with other preparatory acts of devotion: instructions, prayers, examinations, exorcisms (casting out of evil spirits), and so on. All these features have left their mark on the liturgical provisions we use even today, as we shall see. But these additional observances, including the fasting, were as yet required only of the candiates. The rest of the faithful still kept the original one or one-and-a-half day fast.

Thus to the end of the second century there were, so to speak, two "Lents" (the very use of the word is of course at this time an anachronism)—the Lent of the faithful and the Lent of the candidates for baptism.

The third root of our modern Lent lies in the long process by which the faithful took over from the catechumens or candidates under instruction their prebaptismal exercises. Probably this development was due to the cessation of adult baptism as the normal practice. Children were now baptized without having ever gone through the preparatory discipline of the catechumens' Lent—the fasting, exorcisms, and instruction. Since most adult Christians had by now missed that experience, why should they

---

[4] In the second century Church order the bishop was the normal presiding minister in a congregation, assisted by presbyters and deacons.

17

not go through it every year as a preparation for the Easter festival? So the original day or two fast of the faithful was extended, just as the period of preparation for baptism undergone by the catechumens had been extended at an earlier date. Hence, the canons or Church rules drawn up for the first time by the Council of Nicea (A.D. 325), according to the most probable interpretation, mention a Lent lasting for forty days. More certain references occur some years later in the pastoral letters of St Athanasius, written each year at Epiphany to prepare the faithful for the coming season of Lent and Easter. But the length of Lent varied from place to place. The forty days were variously calculated, depending on whether Saturdays were included or not (Sundays of course were always left out of reckoning). Sometimes Lent lasted for more than forty days but often for less. Even today the reckoning is by no means uniform. In the Eastern Churches the fast is spread out over eight or nine weeks, while in the Ambrosian liturgy (still used in the diocese of Milan and therefore by Pope Paul VI while he was archbishop there), Lent starts on the First Sunday in Lent. The Anglican Communion follows what came to be the normal custom in the West, beginning Lent four days earlier than the first Sunday, namely on Ash Wednesday.

From about the fourth to the eighth century there were still catechumens preparing for baptism. Hence it was still realized that during Lent the faithful were sharing the disciplines of the catechumens, their instruction, prayer and fasting. While the catechumens were preparing for baptism, the faithful were preparing for the paschal feast, and particularly for the paschal eucharist. They were "beginning all over again". They were putting themselves back into the catechumenate, as it were. But in course of time, there were fewer catechumens and fewer Easter baptisms. So gradually this idea that the faithful were sharing the disciplines of the catechumens was forgotten. Some other rationale for Lent was needed to take its place. This was found in the penitential system. Just as, earlier, the faithful had taken over the discipline of the catechumens, so now at a later stage they took over the discipline of the penitents.

The origins of the penitential system are wrapped in obscurity.

But we do know that by the third century there had emerged a system of dealing with grievous sin. Anyone who had fallen into such sin was given a chance to work his passage back to good standing in the Church. First, after public (and later private) confession of his sins, he was enrolled among the penitents. He wore a special robe, his hair was cropped close, and at the Sunday eucharist he occupied a special place near the back of the church, between the catechumens and the faithful. He was excluded from taking communion, and received instead only a laying on of hands from the bishop each Sunday. Meanwhile he underwent a rigorous diet of prayer, fasting, and almsgiving. After he was deemed to have done a proper penance he was restored to good standing by receiving absolution. It would seem that at Rome before the eighth century this process of penance was connected with the developing season of Lent. Ash Wednesday was the day in which the penitents were first enrolled. The penance itself lasted through Lent, and the penitents received absolution and restoration on Maundy Thursday, in time for the paschal festival.

Like the earlier system of the catechumenate, this public penitential system also fell into disuse. In place of it, all the faithful were, so to speak, enrolled as the penitents on Ash Wednesday by receiving the imposition of ashes. Thus enrolled, they underwent in a milder form the penitential disciplines of earlier times—prayer, fasting, and almsgiving. Instead of being a brief period of fasting in preparation for the great feast of our redemption (as in earlier times); instead, too, of being a participation in the instructions and devotions of the catechumens; Lent now became a period of almost unrelieved mourning for sin. This penitential concept of Lent was dominant in the middle ages. It was what the Reformers inherited and made the major theme of Lent in the Book of Common Prayer. If, however, we dig deep enough we shall find that the older ideas of Lent (instruction and preparation for Easter) are also there, and we should certainly make more of these than we customarily do.

19

The Development of Passiontide and Holy Week

In order to complete the picture of the development of Lent as we have it today we must go back a bit and take a look at the development of Holy Week. As we saw earlier in this chapter, the primitive Church from New Testament times down to the fourth century observed a single paschal festival which "commemorated" or "celebrated" (in the biblical sense) the great mystery of our redemption. This mystery included the incarnation, life, death, resurrection, ascension of our Lord, the coming of the Holy Spirit, and the anticipated return of Christ.

During the fourth century the original paschal feast was split up into its constituent parts. This happened at Jerusalem; understandably so, for the Jerusalem Church possessed the sacred sites at which the events in the last days of the Lord's life had (allegedly at least) transpired. The Emperor Constantine had taken a great interest in these sites. Churches had been built to commemorate the various events. It was apparently an enterprising and imaginative local leader, Cyril of Jerusalem, who exploited the possibilities of these sites, and the ease of travel in the Roman Empire after the peace of the Church under Constantine made it possible for pilgrims to flock to the Holy Land from all parts of the Christian world.

Each day was observed with a special commemoration in the church at the appropriate site. These observances are described in a fascinating account by a Spanish nun, Etheria, who made the pilgrimage in A.D. 385. On the second Sunday before Easter (which we now call Passion Sunday) there was a procession to Bethany where the story of the raising of Lazarus was read. Then, a week later, there was Palm Sunday, in the afternoon of which the pilgrims made their way to the Mount of Olives, and returned in procession to the city of Jerusalem carrying branches of palm. On the evenings of Monday, Tuesday, and Wednesday there were special services commemorating Jesus' withdrawal to Bethany every night. On Maundy Thursday there was an evening celebration of the Lord's Supper in commemoration of the Upper Room. Then there was an all-night vigil, first in the church on the Mount of Olives, and later in Gethsemane. Then, in the early morning of Good Friday, the pilgrims returned to the city for the reading of the story of Jesus' trial. Later on in the morning there took place the veneration of the relics of the true cross, and a watch was kept at Golgotha from 12 noon until 3 p.m., commemorating the three hours' darkness. In the evening the pilgrims adjourned to the Holy Sepulchre for the reading of the story of Jesus' burial. The paschal feast with its preceding vigil took place the next day, lasting into the midnight of Saturday-Sunday. It was conducted very much according to earlier practices but with one important difference. The feast itself now celebrated not the whole redemption in Christ but only his resurrection from the grave.

All this was not merely a change and development in liturgical arrangements, or an elaboration of the Church year. It represented also a profound change in the whole attitude to commemoration. It involved the loss of the older biblical idea of commemoration as reliving and participating in the mystery of our redemption, and the substitution of the idea we still have today of the purely historical commemoration of past events, the mental recalling of them. While we may not now see fit to go back to the older, single feast of our redemption, at least we must try to get back to the older biblical idea of commemoration as reliving and participating in the total mystery, with special accent no doubt on one of the separate mysteries on each specific occasion.

One further point, however, needs to be noticed. As Lent has developed, it is not only a preparation, devotional, instructional, and penitential, for the paschal mystery. The paschal mystery itself, as originally understood, now occupies the last two weeks in Lent—for from Passion Sunday (and still more clearly from Palm Sunday on) we turn from the earlier themes of penitence, instruction, and devotional preparation to an actual commemoration of the mighty acts of our redemption.

To many modern Church people the idea of six-and-a-half weeks of Lent seems unduly long. Some look back wistfully to the three week Lent of the catechumens, or even to the one or two day Lent of the primitive faithful. If, however, we bear in mind the whole history of the season, and the various associations which have gathered around it at different periods, we shall find enough variety and enough profit from all of them, and six-and-a-half weeks need not then seem too long or too monotonous.

Lent, then, as we have it today, in the light of the history of its development, comprises three main purposes. In the order of their chronological development they are:

1. Preparation for and transition into the paschal mystery.

2. A refresher course of instruction with the catechumens.

3. A reminder of our sinfulness and a renewal of penitence.

Since each of these three motifs was added on to Lent backwards (the two day Lenten preparation for Easter, then the three week Lent of instruction, then finally the six-and-a-half week Lent combining 1, 2, and 3 respectively) we shall approach each of these three motifs in reverse order. In the first part of Lent the emphasis will be on penitence; in the second part, on instruction in the fundamental Christian doctrines and ethics; in the third part, on preparation for and transition into the paschal mystery. We shall seek to show how the "propers" (i.e. the liturgical readings and prayer appointed for the seasons) reflect in turn the three motifs, which have come down from the various periods in the season's history.

3

LENT AND PENITENCE

ASH WEDNESDAY

Nowhere is Lent prescribed in holy Scripture. Later on the Church sought scriptural precedents for the forty days' fasting— the forty days Moses spent in the mount, the forty days Elijah spent in the wilderness, and again the Saviour's forty days' fasting and temptation. All these precedents, though they figure in some early Latin hymns[1] were very much an afterthought.. In no sense can they be quoted as actually enjoining the keeping of Lent, as the words of institution at the Last Supper are quoted as our authority for celebrating the eucharist. Unless one yields to the Puritan insistence that everything that is not directly prescribed in holy Scripture is unallowable in the Church (a point of view that Anglicans have consistently rejected) this does not mean that Lent is unscriptural. Lent was a way devised in the Church to implement its obedience to the gospel. We may well believe that the Church in devising it was guided by the Holy Spirit.

Lent, as we saw in the previous chapter, grew out of the early Christian paschal feast, the celebration of the events of our redemption, particularly the death and resurrection of our Lord Jesus Christ. This is the centre and very heart of the gospel: "[He] was put to death for our trespasses and raised for our justification" (Rom. 4. 25).

Although the gospel asserts most emphatically that this decisive event of our redemption happened once and for all in

[1] See "The glory of these forty days", *English Hymnal*, No. 68 (6th century), with its references to the fasts of Christ, Moses, Elijah, Daniel, and John the Baptist.

23

the past, nevertheless it asserts equally emphatically that we, the recipients of this redemption, have to participate in it ever anew. This participation started with our baptism (and it will be remembered from the last chapter that baptism was particularly associated with the paschal festival in the early Church):

> Do you not know that all of us who have been baptized into Christ Jesus were baptized into his death? We were buried therefore with him by baptism into death, so that as Christ was raised from the dead by the glory of the Father, we too might walk in newness of life.
>
> For if we have been united with him in a death like his, we shall certainly be united with him in a resurrection like his. We know that our old self was crucified with him so that the sinful body might be destroyed, and we might no longer be enslaved to sin. For he who has died is freed from sin. But if we have died with Christ we believe that we shall also live with him. For we know that Christ being raised from the dead will never die again; death no longer has dominion over him. The death he died he died to sin, once for all, but the life he lives he lives to God. So you also must consider yourselves dead to sin and alive to God in Christ Jesus (Rom. 6. 3-11).

Yes, we did die with Christ in our baptism. But all the verbs which speak of our rising to newness of life are either in the future or in the subjunctive or imperative: "so we *might* walk in newness of life"; we *shall certainly* be united with him in a resurrection like his; "we *shall* also live with him"; "you also *must consider* yourselves dead to sin . . . and alive to God". In other words, our dying to sin and rising to newness of life is never—on this side of the second coming—an assured possession. We can never rest on our laurels and say that we are there, that we are saved.

Of course, there is one sense in which this is true. The question of the Salvation Army lassie, "Are you saved?", had a point. We *were* saved when we committed ourselves to Christ in our baptism (or when the commitment was made for us by our sponsors and we took the commitment upon ourselves in confirmation). In our baptism we were actually made "a member of Christ, the child of God, and an inheritor of the kingdom of heaven.[2]

2 BCP Catechism (American BCP, p. 283).

24

But although this was done once and for all in our baptism, sacramentally and objectively, we have to "become what we are". This notion of becoming what we are is not really a strange one, though it may look like it at first sight. Consider a young man who has been drafted into the army. He becomes a soldier and receives his country's uniform. He walks down Main Street on his first night off. Everybody who sees him says to himself, "There goes a soldier". But put him straight away in the front line of battle and it will be immediately obvious that he is any-thing but a soldier. Although he has all the outward, objective status of a soldier he is not yet one subjectively, in his very being. He must first undergo a strenuous period of training. He must become what he is. So it is with the Christian. All through his life he must be for ever becoming what he is. The indicative, as Bultmann has put it, implies an imperative. The indicative says, "You are a Christian". The imperative says, "You must become a Christian, you must become what you are. You must die daily to sin in order to arise to newness of life". As Luther used to insist, we must "die every day" (1 Cor. 15. 31). Yet, what we should always do we often fail to do at all because at no time do we make a special effort to do it. Lent is the season when the Church in her wisdom calls upon us to make just that special effort.

Readers of Dietrich Bonhoeffer's *Letters and Papers from Prison* will remember that Bonhoeffer considered Repentance Day (a Wednesday in November, an occasion in German Luther-anism similar to Ash Wednesday) as the appropriate occasion for the performance of Bach's Mass in B Minor:

While I am writing this letter on Repentance Day, the S[chleicher]s are all listening to the Mass in B minor. For years now I have associated it with this particular day, like the St Matthew Passion with Good Friday. I well remember the evening when I first head it. I was eighteen and had just come from Harnack's Seminar in which he had discussed my first Seminar essay very kindly and had expressed the hope that some day I should specialize in Church History. I was full of this when I went into the Philharmonic Hall; the great *Kyrie Eleison* was just beginning, and, as it did so, I forgot everything else—

25

its effect was indescribable. (*Letters and Papers from Prison* [London, 1967], p. 73)

Of this same music Sir Edwyn Hoskyns has also written, quite independently:

> When John Sebastian Bach sought to give musical expression to the very kernel of Christian truth, he turned to the Mass for his words. The B Minor Mass opens with the poignant cry of the whole chorus and orchestra, Kyrie eleison, Lord, have mercy, and in the fugue which follows all the voices and instruments independently take up the theme: there are no other words, simply Kyrie eleison (*Cambridge Sermons*, [London, 1938], p. 87).

The cry, *Kyrie eleison* is the ground bass of the Christian life. But it is especially accentuated at the beginning of Lent, and that is why Bonhoeffer considered Bach's B Minor Mass as especially appropriate to a day of Repentance. Luther showed the same insight when he described the Christian as *simul justus et peccator*, righteous and sinner, both at the same time. Lent reminds us that we are each of us *peccator*, a sinner, as well as *justus*, righteous: sinners in ourselves, though righteous before God through Jesus Christ.

There are of course some who would like to scrap the penitential emphasis in Lent. They point out, rightly enough as we saw in the last chapter, that the penitential emphasis is the latest and least important of Lent's associations. It is true also that in the Middle Ages, and even after the Reformation, in Anglican tradition, the penitential aspect has been over-emphasized to the exclusion of the earlier aspects of Lent, the preparation for the paschal festival of redemption, and the refresher course in Christian doctrine and ethics. But it will not do to abolish the penitential aspect altogether, nor to soft-pedal it, nice and jolly though that may seem to be to our easygoing modern world. The insights of Luther, Bonhoeffer, and Sir Edwyn Hoskyns—as well as that "fifth Evangelist", Johann Sebastian Bach—forbid us to do that. Most of all, the New Testament forbids it. So, as we shall see, does the liturgy.

Instead, we must try to get penitence into focus. We must

balance it by the other two emphases of Lent, the preparation for participation in the paschal mystery and the refresher course in Christian doctrine and ethics. An examination of the liturgical "propers" suggests that the penitential emphasis is uppermost on Ash Wednesday. Then from Lent I to III inclusive the dominant theme is sharing the instruction of the catechumens. The week of Lent IV serves as an interlude, and then on Lent V (Passion Sunday) we embark upon the participation in the mysteries of the passion and resurrection. Divided up in this way, Lent ceases to be too long or boring, as some people complain, but retains the three emphases which it acquired in the course of its earlier development.

So we begin with the penitential aspect of Lent and turn to a consideration of the liturgical propers for Ash Wednesday.

Ash Wednesday: The Collect

According to most experts, the word "collect" originally meant a prayer said at the beginning of the service, at the time when all the people were "collected" together. It is perhaps more helpful nowadays to use the word somewhat differently, namely as a prayer which *collects* up all the prayers of the Church on a particular day, though its history may not justify it. The original Latin collect appointed for Ash Wednesday had been concerned more about fasting. The BCP collect, which was probably composed by Cranmer for the first English Prayer Book of 1549, shifts attention to the more important theme of penitence. It borrows some thoughts from the prayers in the old service for the imposition of the ashes (e.g., "who hatest nothing that thou hast made"), and weaves in other thoughts from Psalm 51, the chief of the penitential psalms ("create and make in us new and contrite hearts").

The double source of this collect suggests two ideas. First, in Lent we are placing ourselves in the position of the penitents in the ancient Church, who on this day were enrolled among those under discipline and had to work their passage back in time for Easter. Most of us have not committed the heinous sins that merited temporary exclusion from Communion, but all of us

27

nevertheless are sinners. The overt symptoms may be milder, but the basic disease is the same—our self-centredness, which colours even our right actions: "all our righteous deeds are like a polluted garment" (Isa. 64. 6).

Secondly, according to tradition, Psalm 51 was the psalm which David used after Nathan had confronted him with his sin when the king engineered the death of Uriah the Hittite so that he could marry Bathsheba (2 Sam. 11. 2-12, 15). This episode is very instructive for the way it deals with sin. First, Nathan confronts David with his violation of God's law (2 Sam. 12. 1-12), and so stabs his conscience wide awake. In a similar way we have to be confronted by the law of God, in order that we may see ourselves in its mirror for what we are. The Lutheran *Formula of Concord* of 1570[3] speaks here of the "first use of the law", God's law, as a summons to repentance. The same conception of the law's function is present in the rubric in the BCP before the Decalogue: "Then shall the Priest . . . rehearse . . . the Ten Commandments . . . The people . . . shall after every commandment ask God mercy for their transgressions thereof in the past". Unless we examine our consciences in the light of God's law, our expressions of penitence in the liturgy will be no more than an indulgence of emotion. We have to be concrete and practical about penitence. When David had been stabbed wide awake in conscience, he exclaimed: "I have sinned against the Lord" (2 Sam. 12. 13). *"Against the Lord"*—not just against his own self-respect, not only against Uriah and Bathsheba, but against the Lord. This is what the collect means when it speaks of a "new and *contrite* heart"—contrition, as opposed to attrition (remorse): *"against thee, thee only, have I sinned, and done that which is evil in thy sight"* (Ps. 51. 4). Contrition thus leads straight to confession: "I have sinned against the Lord"— "against thee *have I sinned*". Confession is the expression of contrition. So, too, the Ash Wednesday collect: ". . . that we, worthily lamenting our sins, and acknowledging our wretchedness". Why "worthily"? Is there any suggestion here that our penitence may somehow merit God's forgiveness? Not at all: "worthily" here means "in a manner befitting our sinfulness"

[3] See A. R. Vidler, *Christ's Strange Work* (London, 1942), pp. 21f.

28

(Latin: *condigne*), lamenting, as our sins deserve that we should. "Worthily lamenting our sins and acknowledging our wretchedness"—is this saying the same thing twice over as Hebrew poetry so often does? (Cf. "I know my transgressions and my sin is ever before me" (Ps. 51. 3, on which this phrase is probably based). Perhaps so. But probably Cranmer, or whoever wrote the collect, wanted to draw a distinction here: "sins" are the actual, concrete offences we have committed. "Wretchedness" denotes an underlying disease, of which the "sins" are the symptom. This is what the theologians have called original sin, that "infection of nature" which remains even "in them that are regenerated" (Article IX). Lastly comes the goal of self-examination, contrition, and confession: "that we may obtain perfect remission and forgiveness". Nathan says to David after his confession "The Lord has put away thy sin". Nathan pronounces absolution, he assures the penitent that God has granted him perfect remission and forgiveness. David is restored to a right relationship with God. But if it is "perfect", the restored relationship must lead to amendment of life. As Jesus said to the woman taken in adultery, "Go, and do not sin again" (John 8. 11).

If the collect of Ash Wednesday is to mean anything, if it is not to go in one ear and out of the other, then at some time during Lent—and if we are to keep in tune with the liturgy it should be during the early part of the season—we should submit ourselves to this discipline: (1) self-examination in the light of God's law; (2) contrition; (3) confession; (4) absolution; (5) resolution to amend our lives.

We *must* do this. How or when is left to ourselves. We ought to know that if we mean business about it, there is in our Anglican tradition, retained at the Reformation, an opportunity to do this in a particularly concrete though not necessarily very pleasant way. And sin is after all not a very pleasant thing!

Luther wrote: "Private confession . . . though it cannot be proved from Scripture, is wholly commendable, useful and indeed necessary. I would not have it cease, but rather I rejoice that it exists in the Church of Christ, for it is the one and only remedy for troubled consciences" (*The Babylonish Captivity of the Church*, v. 16).

And without apology he included in his short catechism (section five): "How the simple folks should be taught to confess". He goes on taking it for granted that this will be done to a confessor, giving a form for so doing.

The Book of Common Prayer similarly includes this invitation:

> . . . if there be any of you, who by this means [namely, by self-examination and direct confession to God] cannot quiet his own conscience herein, but requireth further comfort or counsel, let him come to me, or to some other discreet and learned Minister of God's Word, and open his grief [i.e., make his confession]; that by the ministry of God's holy Word, he may receive the benefit of absolution, together with ghostly counsel and advice . . . .[4]

What is the advantage of this particular discipline? First, it forces us to be perfectly definite over the confession of our sins. It is easy to confess quite generally our past sinfulness without being specific about it. If we make an appointment to confess, it forces us systematically to examine ourselves in the light of the commandments.

Secondly—and this was a point which weighed heavily with Bonhoeffer in his protest against "cheap grace"—it is so easy to pronounce our own absolution, to "kid ourselves" into thinking we are forgiven, instead of hearing it come as a word from outside ourselves. "Cheap grace is the preaching of forgiveness without requiring repentance . . . Communion without confession, absolution without personal confession" (D. Bonhoeffer, *The Cost of Discipleship* [London, 1959], p. 36). Later in the same book Bonhoeffer writes:

> There is also the sacramental confession, wherein the Christian seeks and finds assurance that his sins are forgiven. Confession is the God-given remedy for self-deception and self-indulgence. When we confess our sins before a brother Christian we are mortifying the pride of the flesh and delivering it up to shame and death through Christ. Then through the word of absolution we arise as new men, utterly dependent on the mercy of God. Confession is thus a genuine part of the life of the saints, and

[4] It is to be regretted that the American BCP omits the reference to the "benefit of absolution".

one of the gifts of grace . . . "When I admonish men to come to confession, I am simply urging them to be Christians" (Luther, *Great Catechism*), ibid., p. 260ff.

He returns to this subject in a later work:

> Since the confession of sin is made in the presence of a Christian brother, the last stronghold of self-justification is abandoned (D. Bonhoeffer, *Life Together*, [New York, 1954] p. 112).

Thirdly, private confession and absolution provides a very real opportunity for pastoral counselling, directly tailored to the individual's needs, such as cannot be done from the pulpit. It is the difference between reading a medical article in the *Readers' Digest* and running off to the chemist's on the one hand, and going to the doctor for a personal diagnosis and prescription on the other.

Ash Wednesday: The Old Testament Lesson

The Old Testament lesson for Ash Wednesday which now takes the place of an epistle comes from Joel 2. 12-17. Compared with the collect it strikes a different note. There the thought, quite rightly, was primarily of individual repentence, which is always a part, and indeed an essential part, of Lenten concern. But the epistle widens the horizon of penitence. It is *the whole people of God* who are submitting themselves to the Lenten discipline. "Let the priests and the people weep before the altar". As the late Dom Gregory Dix has pertinently written of the time when Lent first developed as an exercise of the faithful as well as of the catechumens:

> The importance of Lent lay precisely in this, that it was not just one more ascetic exercise for the devout, but that it was recognized as being of *universal* obligation. Those who wished might continue to pray and to fast with fervour at other seasons; the sanctity of the Church as a whole might help to carry a considerable number of slack Christians. But Lent was intended to be a strictly *corporate* effort of the whole Church, from the bishop down to the humblest catechumen, to live at least for a season as befitted the Body of Christ—in fervent and frequent

31

prayer and in a serious and mortified spirit, in order that at their corporate Easter communion all might be found truly members of the Body.[5]

All this is easily said. But this is not enough. It is not simply that all of us individuals are in this thing together. It is that the local congregation precisely as a congregation, as the local manifestation of the Body of Christ, is called upon to undergo genuinely *corporate* self-examination, contrition, confession, and amendment. "Let the Church be the Church" is a common slogan today. Lent is a time for the local church, not as a collection of individuals only, but precisely as a congregation, as *the* Church in its particular locality, to ask itself, how far is it being the Church? How far is it fulfilling its mission in the place where it is set? What indeed is its mission in that place? What is its mission in relation to a divided Christendom, its ecumenical task? (The weakness of the ecumenical movement, it is often said, is at the grass roots.) What is its mission in relation to the specific social problems of the neighbourhood, e.g., to its inter-racial problems? What is its mission to those in its locality who deny the faith of Christ crucified or who know not God as he is revealed in the gospel of his Son: in other words in relation to the task of evangelism? What is its mission in relation to the world-wide mission of the Church?

Since the mid-nineteenth century it has been a favourite Lenten activity to hold additional week-night meetings in our parishes. These meetings usually take the form of extra devotional services with hortatory addresses of the usual kind, or (as is common in the U.S.A.) of a family supper, followed by adult, youth, and children's classes of instruction in Christian faith and ethics. The most valuable Lenten programme of this kind in which the present writer ever participated was a modification of the latter type. Here we all met together first as a congregation to study the problems of the Church at Corinth as indicated in 1 Corinthians. Then we split up into groups to apply these insights of St Paul to the local situation, reported back at this end in a plenary session. It would be wonderful if the whole parish could review its mission in this way, and come to a real, corporate

[5] op. cit., p. 357, italics mine.

32

repentance and amendment in respect of its concrete mission in its neighbourhood and locality. Here would be a modern way of implementing the challenge of the epistle: "Blow the trumpet in Zion; santify a fast; call a solemn assembly; gather the people. Santify the congregation; . . . Between the vestibule and the altar let the priests, the ministers of the Lord, weep and say, 'Spare thy people, O Lord, and make not thy heritage a reproach' ".

Ash Wednesday: The Gospel

The American Prayer Book (p. li) designates Ash Wednesday (together with Good Friday) as "major fasts," noting also that the forty days of Lent are included among "other days of fasting on which the Church requires such a measure of abstinence as is more especially suited to extraordinary acts and exercises of devotion."

Modern Christians have little use for the old-fashioned practice of fasting. This feeling began at the Reformation, as a natural revolt against the elaborate rules of the medieval Church which smacked too much of "good works", done for merit. But the Reformers never intended to abolish fasting as such. After all, the New Testament takes it for granted that fasting is a part of the Christian life. There are plenty of examples of fasting in the first three centuries after the Reformation. Days of "humiliation and fasting" used to be appointed by the civil authority both in Britain and America in times of calamity and distress. It is, one fears, the modern wordliness of Protestantism in an affluent society which has allowed these older practices to go entirely by the board. It is part of the "cheap grace" about which Bonhoeffer protested so vigorously. It is a mistaken application of the principle of justification by faith alone.

Assuming, then, that the Churches (with Jesus himself and the New Testament) expect us to fast, how, concretely, shall we do it? One of the most relevant types of fasting in the modern world—a type incidentally practised by agnostics and humanists among university students—is to live for a day as people in undeveloped countries, or at least have the same kind of meal they have, and to give to a famine relief fund the money which would have been spent normally on that day or for that meal. Traditionally, fasting went with almsgiving as well as with prayer, and here is a modern way of effecting the combination.

The gospel of Ash Wednesday is concerned not with methods of fasting, but with its motivation. It says that fasting is not to be undertaken in order to be "seen of men", but is to be done in secret, in the eyes of God. Thus the gospel rules out in advance any idea of fasting to acquire merit. Not even the promise of a reward from the heavenly Father intends to suggest that. It means that fasting will bear fruit, fruit in a detachment from the things of this world for their own sake, and in a genuine commitment to God.

The last three verses of the gospel ("Do not lay up for your-selves treasures on earth . . .") make this plain. There is no suggestion in this detachment from the world that the things of this world are in themselves evil, as Manicheeism and, much later, pietistic Puritanism have taught. That would be quite contrary to biblical doctrine from the first chapter of Genesis on. God made the things of this world and saw that they were good. The trouble, however, is that man, being a fallen sinner, is always tempted to worship the creature instead of the creator, to treat the penultimate[6] things of life as though they were ultimates. So in fasting we detach ourselves for a season from the penultimates in order that we may attach ourselves to him who is Ultimate. Then, in due course we shall receive back the things that are penulti-mate, no longer mistaking them for ultimates, but knowing precisely that they are just that—penultimates, accepting them gratefully as a gift from God, and using them responsibly in accordance with his will. That is partly why Christian fasting is seasonal, not (as in latter-day Puritanism) perennial. We abstain not from evils, but from goods, in order to learn that they are precisely goods, not gods.

6 This distinction between ultimate and penultimate was introduced into modern theology and ethics by D. Bonhoeffer. See his *Ethics* (New York, 1965), pp. 120-187.

34

4

LENT AND LEARNING

LENT 1–3

Penitence, as we have seen, is the ground-bass of the Christian life. It therefore remains the ground-bass of Lent, as we are occasionally reminded in the propers. But it is only in the propers for Ash Wednesday that there is exclusive concentration upon the theme of penitence.

Lent 1 (Invocabit[1]): The Collect

The ancient (Latin) Collect appointed for Lent 1 ran thus:

> O God, who dost purify thy Church by the yearly observance of Lent; Grant unto thy household that it may pursue in good works that which it strives to obtain from thee by abstinence . . ..

Obviously, the Reformers could not accept this collect's suggestion that fasting was a good work and a means of acquiring merit. So they composed a new collect of their own, which however retained the ancient theme of fasting.

Fasting, as we saw in Chapter 1, is among other things a natural expression of penitence. But we have a further thought. Fasting or abstinence[2] is also a means of subduing the flesh to

[1] The traditional Latin names for the Sundays from Lent 1 to Pentecost represent the first word(s) of the ancient Introit. These names are in common popular use among Roman Catholics and Lutherans, and will be found in the *English Hymnal* (Nos. 676-690).

[2] The older tradition made no distinction between fasting and abstinence. It was only in 1781 that the Roman Church distinguished

the Spirit. Note the capital S here. It is not the subduing of our lower nature, by our (supposedly) higher nature. Such an idea is unbiblical. Our whole nature, in the biblical perspective, was created good, but our whole nature, mind and spirit as well as body, has been corrupted by sin. By fasting we learnt to say "No" to self, the self which is the root of our sin, and therefore become more ready to say "Yes" to God and his will, to obey the godly "motions" or promptings of his Holy Spirit, and so attain to a life of righteousness and true holiness. Thus the BCP collect stresses that penitential exercises such as fasting are meant to lead to practical amendment of life. They are not just the indulgence of emotion.

In passing, before we leave this collect, it should be noted how the opening clause alludes to the gospel of the day, the story of the Lord's temptations: "O God, who for our sake didst fast forty days and forty nights." No doubt the Anglican Reformers were here seeking scriptural justification or at least precedent for the forty days' fast of Lent. But that, as we have seen, was very much an afterthought, of which we are tempted to make too much, perhaps because of the popular Lenten hymn, "Forty days and forty nights".

THE LENTEN EPISTLES : LENT 1-3

Our present Lenten Sunday epistles and gospels are the relics of a daily series of scriptural readings. These originally served as a course of instructions for the catechumens. Their subject was Christian faith and morals. Later these lessons were intended also for the penitents who were under discipline. That is why the Sunday epistles as we now have them draw a contrast between the old pagan life, which the recent converts had previously shared and which they knew only too well, and the Christian life upon which they were now embarking.

between "fasting" (=going without food of any kind) and "abstinence" (=going without flesh meat). But in the collect abstinence has a larger sense than fasting: "it does not limit the means of self denial to one particular way" (M. Shepherd, *The Oxford American Prayer Book Commentary* [New York, 1950], pp. 125-6).

36

Lent 1: The Epistle (2 Cor. 6. 1-10)

Paul is speaking in the fullness of his apostolic authority—"working together with [him]". The word "him" (i.e. God) is not in the original Greek, which simply means "co-operating". Co-operating with whom? we naturally ask. It *could* mean Paul co-operating with his companions, an interpretation which has been suggested sometimes by those who are afraid of the idea of "co-operating" with God. We stumble here on an old Reformation controversy. Melanchthon maintained that, in attaining to justifying faith, man's will co-operates with the grace of God, a view which was dubbed "synergism". Melanchthon held that man contributed 1% and God 99%—as against Pelagianism which gave man 100%, and medieval scholasticism which settled for 50/50. The proper answer is to be sought in terms of the Pauline paradox, "I, yet not I, but Christ in me" (see Gal. 2. 20; 1 Cor. 15. 10). In other words, man does 100% but paradoxically this 100% is entirely the work of God's grace. St Paul is talking in our epistle, however, not of the Christian life in general but of his apostolic mission, in which, as the Saviour promised, "He that heareth you heareth me", in which he laboured more abundantly than they all, yet not he but the grace of God which was in him. Paul and God (or Christ) co-operate not in the sense that they each contribute 50/50, but in the sense that Paul labours entirely and completely, and yet it is not he, but the grace of God in him.

The apostles are now dead, but their work lives on in the New Testament which preserves their witness. And the Church is apostolic because she makes that witness a living voice today in her accredited ministry. So we hear the word of the Lord, spoken originally by Paul to his converts at Corinth, spoken later by the Church to the catechumens, still later by the Church to the penitent, and now to the congregation today as it embarks upon the liturgical observance of Lent.

Let us for a moment recall the catechumens, for whom this epistle was first chosen in liturgical usage. They are standing on the brink of the decisive moment of their lives. On Easter Eve they will be baptized, they will receive the grace of God—i.e. the

37

saving act of God in Christ will become present to them—and they will be incorporated in the new Israel. But it is possible for them to receive the grace of God "in vain". Their baptism is not to be a magic ceremony, automatically guaranteeing their salvation. It must be followed by the sustained response of obedience.

Paul, as he often does, reinforces his plea with a scriptural quotation (from Isa. 49. 8):

> In a time of favour I have answered you,
> in a day of salvation I have helped you.

To this quotation Paul adds his own application: *Now* is the time of favour. *Now* is the day of salvation. By the "now" he meant the new age of fulfilment inaugurated by the death and resurrection of Christ, the age of the preaching of the gospel by the apostles. For the catechumens, the "now" meant the time of their preparation for and receiving of baptism. In the liturgy "now" means the season of Lent. In this Lenten season, in the readings of scripture which the liturgy provides, in the eucharistic celebrations, culminating in the great eucharist of the paschal feast, is the Now. Lent is not just an easygoing cultic observance, but an urgent confrontation with our eternal destiny, the opportunity to choose "Now" to accept the grace of God, and to accept it not in vain. Thus the epistle of Lent I "is in the nature of a general introduction to the season" (M. Shepherd, op. cit., p. 126-127).

From this point in the epistle Paul speaks of his own apostolic labours. What follows is not directly or at first sight what we should expect, namely, an exhortation to the converts about their own Christian living. (For Paul ought to have gone on to show precisely what it meant to offer a sustained response of obedience). But in the situation in which he wrote his letter, he was not really going off at a tangent, for the Corinthians were succumbing to the blandishments of false apostles who had turned up at Corinth with a perverted gospel. In this version of the gospel they over-emphasized the fact that salvation was a present reality. They claimed that they were in heaven already. There was no need for any moral effort and no place for suffering in the

38

Christian life. Above all, the Christian life for them meant the exercise of spectacular spiritual gifts—visions, ecstatic experiences, speaking with tongues, and the like. Of all this we hear in 2 Cor. 10—13. These spectacular gifts, they claimed, were the signs of a true apostle. They were also the signs of true converts. Paul, they claimed, was not a true apostle because he did not manifest these spectacular gifts in his own ministry. It is in answer to this that Paul stresses not the spectacular things (though he could claim such) but rather what has been called the "cross-side" of the ministry, his apostolic sufferings. To be an apostle is not primarily to have ecstatic visions, or speak with tongues, but to show great endurance, to undergo "afflictions, hardships, calamities, beatings, imprisonments, tumults, labours, watching, hunger". It is these things that show him to be an apostle. For the life of an apostle is conformed entirely to the gospel of the cross. The resurrection-side is not yet. That is to come hereafter, when Christ returns in glory and takes his own to himself.

But although grammatically and logically Paul is speaking here of his apostolic labours, his words also have an indirect reference to the life which his converts are to live. If they underplayed the cross-side of the gospel itself and the cross-side of apostleship, they also underplayed the cross-side in their own Christian living. This is why they were receiving the grace of God in vain. They supposed that to be a Christian meant to enjoy ecstatic experiences and to speak with tongues and to work miracles. Paul is obliquely reminding them that the Christian life—the life of all Christians, and not only the apostles—has its cross-side.

So too the shift to the later situation in the life of the Church, when this lesson was chosen for the catechumens, serves to remind them of what they, too, are being let in for. To be a Christian means to be prepared, like the Apostle, for suffering. It is just as the Lord himself had said: "If anyone would be my disciple, let him take up his cross and follow me". The catechumens were thus reminded of the cost of discipleship on which they were to embark at baptism on Easter Even. And to bring it down to our own situation, the Church is reminded of the cross-side of Christianity at the beginning of Lent, as it prepares to renew its commitment at the paschal feast.

This epistle also comes appropriately at the beginning of an Ember Week, one of the four seasons of the year when prayers are offered for the ordained ministry of the Church. Each of these Ember Seasons lays before us some particular aspect of the Church's ministry.[3] The Lenten Ember Season reminds us of what we have called the "cross-side" of the ministry.

The late Archbishop William Temple once recalled how at Lambeth Palace his father and predecessor as Primate had caused to be inscribed over one of the doors the words, *"Apostolorum nobis vindicamus non honores sed labores"* (We claim for ourselves not the honours of the apostles, but their labours). This is a salutary reminder for a Church which is often tempted to pride itself on its apostolic succession, and thus to fall into the very same temptation which beset Paul's Corinthians.

THE GOSPELS OF LENT 1-3

As we have seen, the epistles of these Sundays are chosen as instructions in Christian ethics for the catechumens preparing for Easter baptism. They must know the standards of behaviour required of them when they are admitted into membership in the Christian Church.

The gospels appear to have a different concern. They are not, as might have been expected, drawn from the Lord's ethical teaching (e.g., from the Sermon on the Mount), but relate incidents in his life. On the first Sunday we read the story of the temptation (Matt. 4. 1-11), on the second Sunday the story of the Canaanitish woman (Matt. 15. 21-28), and on the third Sunday the exorcism of an unclean spirit, followed by a discourse (Luke 11. 14-28). There is a connecting thread between all of these gospels: they all deal with our Lord's conflicts with the devil. This is obvious in the temptation story of Lent 1 and in the Beelzebul controversy of Lent 3. But it is equally true of Lent 2, for the Syro-Phoenician woman's daughter was, we are

3. The Advent Embertide emphasizes the eschatological aspect of the ministry—its work in preparing a people fit for the Lord's coming (see the Collect of Advent III); the Whitsun Embertide emphasizes the ministry as a gift of the Spirit of the ascended Christ to his Church; the autumn Embertide the ripeness of the harvest and the paucity of the labourers.

told, "severely possessed by a demon". Why this preoccupation with the devil and with evil spirits? The answer seems to lie in the fact that the catechumens of the early Church underwent a whole series of exorcisms in preparation for their baptism. What our Lord had done on earth with the demon-possessed he was still continuing in his Church.

The whole notion of demonic possession is strange to the modern world despite the fact that missionaries returning from primitive countries tell us that there demonic possession is still a very real thing. We find it easier nowadays to talk of complexes and neuroses. Can we therefore make anything of these gospels for the first three Sundays in Lent?

Modern scholarship tends to see in the isolated pericopes of the gospels the whole gospel of God's saving act in Christ proclaimed in a nutshell. Each Sunday gospel is precisely a "gospel" —a proclamation of the good news of the saving act of God in Christ. It is as such that they are read in the liturgy, and it is as such that they are meant to be treated in the liturgical sermon. The saving act of God in Christ reaches its culmination in the cross and resurrection, which will be celebrated at Easter. The Sunday gospels in Lent are prefigurations of the central saving act of cross and resurrection. Thus it is helpful to think of the Sunday gospels in Lent as preparing us for the paschal feast by taking aspects of the central saving act of God and inviting us to contemplate it in advance. It is by this approach that we will examine each of the gospels of Lent 1, 2, and 3. In this way we shall be true to the original intention of these gospels, which was to provide instruction for the catechumens in Christian doctrine just as the epistles provide teaching in Christian behaviour.

Lent 1: The Gospel (Matt. 4. 1-11)

The temptation story portrays Jesus as the second Adam, the true Israel, the servant of the Lord.

He is the second Adam. Adam was tempted by Satan in the garden of Eden, "You shall be as God". Satan offered him the forbidden fruit. Adam succumbed to the temptation and fell. Christ as second Adam is approached by Satan with a similar temptation: "If you are the Son of God . . .". But instead of falling he obeys the will of God. It is here that Christ chooses the path that is to lead him to the cross, for the cross is the final outcome of his obedience. What the temptation story reveals to us about the cross is succinctly stated by Paul in Romans 5. 17-19:

> If, because of one man's [i.e., Adam's] trespass, death reigned through that one man, much more will those who receive the abundance of grace and the free gift of righteousness reign in life through the one man Jesus Christ.
>
> Then as one man's trespass led to condemnation for all men, so one man's act of righteousness leads to acquittal and life for all men. For as by one man's disobedience many were made sinners, so by one man's obedience many will be made righteous.

The temptation story together with Paul's comment on it reveals to us that the cross is not just bare fact, certainly not just the execution of a criminal (or of a harmless innocent) upon a gibbet. The cross is the culmination in a life of total commitment and obedience to the will of God. And precisely because it is that, it is the reversal of the fall. For Adam's disobedience involved all his descendants. So, too, Christ's act of obedience involves all who are incorporated into him, into the body of the second Adam, and his obedience forms and moulds the lives of Christians. Thus we, too, through his resistance to temptation, are enabled also to resist. We too can reply:

> Man shall not live by bread alone,
> But by every word that proceeds from the mouth of God.

We, too, can defy the devil with the words:

> You shall not tempt the Lord your God.

We, too, can offer our exclusive worship and service to God:

> You shall worship the Lord your God,
> and him only shall you serve.

Thus the temptation occurred "for us men and for our salvation". Hence we pray in the Litany: "By thy . . . Fasting, and Temptation, Good Lord deliver us". The temptation is not just a biographical episode in the life of a religious hero. It is part of

42

the saving act of God in Christ, revealing to us the meaning of the centre of that saving act, the cross and resurrection.

The temptation reveals Christ as the true Israel. Israel was called out of Egypt to be the son of God (Hos. 11. 1). Israel was tempted in the wilderness forty years and fell at Meribah and Massah (Exod. 17. 1-7; Num. 20. 8-13; note how the temptations of Adam, Israel, and Christ are all concerned with eating and drinking). And each time Christ answers the devil in words taken from the wilderness story (Deut. 8. 3; 6. 16; 6. 13), thus proving himself to be the true Israel, the true servant of the Lord.

It is on the cross finally, deserted and forsaken by all, that Christ hangs as the true Israel. The cross is the centre-point and pivot of salvation history. Henceforth the true Israel is widened out to incorporate Peter, the Twelve, the 500 (1 Cor. 15. 5-6), those in Israel who believe in response to the apostolic word (Rom. 11. 4-5), those among the Gentiles who believe (Rom. 11. 11), till finally the full number of the Gentiles comes in and all Israel shall be saved (Rom. 11. 25-26).

The temptation gospel, chosen though it probably was originally in order to give scriptural sanction for the forty days' fast of Lent, may now serve to confront us with the doctrine of the cross, and to prepare for the approach of Passiontide and Easter. It teaches us that the cross is not just the saving act of God for my own personal salvation, but the turning point of the history of God's dealings with his people. It is the point at which the true Israel is narrowed down to a single man, deserted by his friends, fighting alone the battle against Satan and offering alone the sacrifice of perfect obedience which is demanded of us all. And then because he has won that victory and offered that sacrifice single-handed, we too are enabled in and through him to have the same victory and offer the sacrifice of ourselves, our souls and bodies in obedience to the will of God.

Lent 2 (Reminiscere): The Collect

Many of our Prayer Book collects are petitions for defence from our enemies. These collects come from the troublous times which marked the last days of the Roman Empire, when the barbarians were invading its territories. When those dangers had passed these prayers were retained, but transposed to another key. The "enemies" became not the Huns or the Goths, but the kind of enemy suggested in Eph. 6. 12: "For we are not contending against flesh and blood, but against principalities, against the powers, against the world rulers of this present darkness, against the spiritual hosts of wickedness in the heavenly places." We interpret these collects (Lent 3 is very similar to Lent 2) as we should interpret the so-called imprecatory psalms which caused so much trouble around 1928, when the Revised Prayer Book sought to bracket the offending verses. They were widely regarded as "unchristian", a denial of the teaching of the Sermon on the Mount, to "love your enemies".

In the sixties we are experiencing in many ways a recrudescence of the theological mood of the twenties, and Christians are once more becoming squeamish about the imprecatory psalms and also presumably about the collects which pray in similar vein for deliverance from our enemies. But impatience with this kind of language is not necessarily Christian or biblical. Let us hear what Bonhoeffer has to say about it: [4]

> In so far as Christ is in us, the Christ who took all the vengeance of God upon himself, who met God's vengeance in our stead, who thus stricken—by the wrath of God—and in no other way could forgive his enemies, who himself suffered the wrath that we might go free—we too, as members of Jesus Christ, can pray these psalms, through Jesus Christ, from the heart of Jesus.

Perhaps more helpful is a plea by R. M. Benson, founder of the Society of St John the Evangelist (Cowley Fathers): [5]

> The Comminatory Psalms are therefore essential to the completeness of the Psalter, for without them the mind of Christ, the Redeemer, the Sovereign and the Judge, would not be exhibited to us . . ..
> There must be a real love of God, involving the hatred of evil. These psalms remind us of the strife wherewith the world rages against Christ. It is the strife which we have to share.

[4] D. Bonhoeffer, *Life Together* (London, 1954), p. 147.
[5] R. M. Benson, *War Songs of the Prince of Peace,* (London, 1901) I, 306, 276.

The collect of Lent 2 prays for deliverance from two kinds of enemies, outward "adversities which may happen to the body" as well as "evil thoughts which may assault and hurt the soul". How far is it right for a Christian to pray for deliverance from physical accidents or ailments? It is quite natural that we should do so. Even our Lord prayed in the Garden of Gethsemane to be delivered from his bitter cup. But he added the qualification, "Yet not what I will, but what thou wilt" (Mark 14. 36). And it is always the same qualification, spoken or unspoken, that should accompany such prayers for deliverance from external enemies. This qualification is not an insurance policy against disappointment or to help us make the best of a bad job. It is rather an acknowledgement that the whole purpose of Christian prayer is not our own comfort or convenience, but the promotion of God's will: "Seek ye first his kingdom and his righteousness" (Matt. 6. 33). All else must be subordinated to that. Our prayers for deliverance from illness and danger can only be a prayer that we may be delivered from what, so far as we can see, would be a hindrance to our doing the will of God and to our living our lives in his service. But we must be perfectly ready (as Christ was in Gethsemane) to accept it otherwise if it should be that precisely in and through illness or accident we can serve the Lord as he wills us to serve him.

Lent 2: The Epistle (1 Thess. 4. 1-8)

One of the most striking differences between the old life of paganism from which the catechumens of the ancient Church came, and the new life of the Christian community into which they were entering through baptism, was the different standard of sexual morality.

We get some inkling of the current standards of sexual morality in the pagan world in New Testament times from the letters of St Paul. Tracing this morality (with good reason, for much of it was associated with religion) to its roots in the idolatrous worship of paganism, Paul writes to the Romans complaining:

> God gave them up in the lusts of their hearts to impurity, to the dishonouring of their bodies among themselves . . . For this

reason God gave them up to dishonourable passions. Their women exchanged natural relations for unnatural, and the men likewise gave up natural relations with women and were consumed with passion for one another, men committing shameless acts with men (Romans 1. 24-27).

Here Paul particularly mentions lesbianism and homosexuality among the disorders of the time, and a little later he complains of "fornication" (RSV has squeamishly substituted "improper conduct": Paul calls a spade a spade!). In 1 Cor. 5. 1f he complains that sexual immorality was rife among his own Corinthian converts; a man was living with his father's wife (presumably his young step-mother).

Following the best teaching of the Old Testament Jewish tradition, and the even stricter standards of our Lord himself, the early Church (St Paul included) insisted—for Christians—upon the highest standards the world has ever known: "For this is the will of God . . . that you abstain from immorality; that each one of you know how to take a wife for himself in holiness and honour, not in the passion of lust like heathen who do not know God; that no man transgress, and wrong his brother in this matter . . . For God has not called us for uncleanness, but in holiness" (Thess. 4. 3-7). In other words, Paul sets forth the Christian standard as requiring (1) absolute purity before marriage; (2) life-long monogamy with complete fidelity. This is set forth not as an "ideal" but as the demand of God. Ideals are human standards. They are something to aspire to, though it does not matter all that much if you fall short of them. Better luck next time. If at first you don't succeed, try, try again! With the demand of God, "Thou shalt", it is "woe betide you if you do not: you are condemned as a sinner". This demand is something for all times and all places. Sexual standards may change from age to age: God's demand does not.

What changes is not so much the way men behave as the way they justify their behaviour. In New Testament times, sexual immorality actually claimed the sanction of religion. That is why St Paul can tie it up with idolatry (Rom. 1. 25). The characteristic institution of the day (in the pagan world) was temple prostitution. This had its roots in the ancient fertility cults. To go to a temple and have sexual intercourse with a temple prostitute was regarded as an act of religious devotion— an act of "holy communion". It was not only not sinful, it was positively right and proper.

When we turn to our day, we find a not altogether dissimilar situation. The readers may recall the film *Tom Jones* based on Henry Fielding's novel. Some people were shocked by the standards of behaviour among the upper classes in eighteenth century England. But there was, after all, something rather healthy about eighteenth century bawdiness. At least it didn't try to dress up sin and pretend it was something else. It sinned with great gusto, but still recognized that it was sin. *Pecca fortiter!* Twentieth century immorality (one hesitates to call it "bawdiness" because it lacks the old gusto) sins and pretends that sin is not sin at all, but dresses it up in all sorts of fancy names: "self-expression", "fulfilment", "release from repression", and the like. Such behaviour is called "enlightened", "progressive". Between the eighteenth and twentieth centuries Victorian puritan- ism has supervened. The latter did a good job cleaning up the manners of society, but it has left us with an overwhelming need for self-justification. The odd thing about it is that it is precisely those who are loudest in their rebellion against Victorian morality who are most obviously its products. Instead of sinning and honestly admitting it (like our eighteenth century forebears), they justify it in the name of psychology. Freudianism is a post- Victorian phenomenon. Adultery, fornication, and the rest are now held up to be right and good. "Hypocrisy begins not only when men fail to practise what they preach but also when they begin to preach what they practise."[6]

This is the situation in which the Church today has to pro- claim the demand of God which Paul proclaimed in an age of temple prostitution. We are told by some of the fashionable theological radicals that it is in this situation that the Church can no longer go on repeating a morality which says "this is right, that is wrong". Young people, particularly, are not con- vinced: they want to know "why?", and "why" is a question you

---

[6] Arnold Lunn and Garth Lean, *The New Morality*, (London, 1964), p. 12.

can only answer in the light of a full knowledge of every concrete situation. There is only one absolute Christian command, and that is the command of love.

Of course this is perfectly true. All the commandments are summed up in the one command, "You shall love your neighbour as yourself" (Rom. 13. 9). But the concrete commandments are not *abrogated* in that command. The concrete commandments are simply illustrations of what the commandment of love will mean precisely and concretely in a particular situation. Thus fornication is an infringement, not of some abstract standard of right and wrong but of the commandment of love. Why? Because love means total commitment of oneself to the neighbour and to his welfare. Sexual relations outside lifelong monogamous marriage are always *ipso facto* done in a context where there is less than total commitment. True, there are degrees here—and the Church has often so concentrated on the black and white that it has ignored intermediate shades of grey. It is perhaps *more* in accordance with responsible love to commit fornication with contraceptives than to risk an illegitimate child. It is *more* in accordance with responsible love to have intercourse with the girl to whom you are engaged than with a casual contact. Yet even there the total commitment has not yet been made but only promised. And therefore it is not fully in accord with the great commandment, "You shall *love* your neighbour".

Thus the traditional commandments are still needed. They give practical guidance as to precisely what love does mean in a concrete situation. We have not time in every situation to think out concretely what love means within it. The concrete commandments give us rough and ready guidance as to what love does demand. Of course, there is no suggestion that when we have kept these concrete commandments we have fulfilled all the demands of love. But the full demands of love are always higher—and never lower—than the concrete commands. That was the meaning of Jesus' criticism of the law in the "antitheses" of the Sermon on the Mount, (Matt. 5. 21-48) which contrast with the old law and Jesus' demands; "You have heard that it was said . . . but I say to you".

Yet there is a reluctance on the part of the Church today to speak about such things. We may at least welcome the radical theologians for having forced us to bring the subject again to the fore. Part of the trouble is that in our reaction against the Church's practice in the past we are spending much more time on the *social* evils of our day than on individual sin. It is of course much more exciting and in contemporary mood much more popular to take part in civil rights demonstrations than to preach chastity. But this "you ought to have done, without neglecting the others" (Matt. 23. 23).

Another reason for the soft-pedalling of God's demand in the sexual sphere is what Dr Gibson Winter has called the "suburban captivity of the Churches". We are afraid of being nonconformists to the customs of suburbia. But, unpleasant thought it may be, the New Testament calls precisely for nonconformity at certain points: "Do not be conformed to this world" writes the Apostle, "but be transformed by the renewal of your mind, that you may prove what is the will of God, what is good and acceptable and perfect" (Rom. 12. 2). The sanctification and holiness of which he speaks in the Epistle of Lent 2 imply the same thing.

Yet again, most Christians in the main-line Christian denominations are in reaction against the latter-day Puritanism which until recently dominated our culture, and which tended to regard sex as an evil *per se*. This was a denial of the doctrine of creation. Now we are falling into the opposite extreme, and proclaim that sex is good *per se*. This is a denial of "original sin". The truth is that sex was good as God created it, but sinful man misuses it. It is an instrument which has to be "hallowed and directed aright".

The Lenten provisions in the Liturgy make it impossible for the Church to abdicate her task of proclaiming God's demand in the sphere of sex. "This is the will of God, your sanctification". Sanctification means of course nonconformity in other spheres of life besides sex. But for Paul's converts, as for twentieth century Christians, this is a sphere in which Christian nonconformity becomes evident. What God demands is so different from the current behaviour of the world, and from the ethical and psychological theories with which it rationalizes its behaviour. Paul makes three concrete demands:

49

1. To the unmarried: "abstain from immorality"—i.e., from premarital sexual intercourse. The reason why this demand is made as a concrete application of the commandment of love has been indicated above.

2. To those about to get married: "take a wife in holiness and honour . . . not in the passion of lust". Or, in the words of the Book of Common Prayer, marriage is not to be entered into "unadvisedly, lightly, or wantonly" but "reverently, discreetly, soberly, and in the fear of God". Marriage is not legalized prostitution, as the radical theologians are rightly reminding us.

3. To those who are married, a warning against adultery: "That no man transgress, and wrong his brother in this matter" (i.e., in the matter of marriage, by running off with another man's wife).

These injunctions are reinforced with a solemn warning, re-iterated from Paul's original instructions to them when they were first prepared for baptism: "The Lord is an avenger in all these things". We are all of us tempted to think that sexual indulgence doesn't matter. We shall get away with it. Not so Paul. In view of the misery and unhappiness in the world today as a result of our so-called progressive morality and the ominous parallels with the decline of the Roman Empire, who can gainsay him?

Finally Paul reminds the Thessalonians of the motive of all Christian behaviour: once again, it is a matter of "Become what you are". We were made holy in our baptism, therefore we must be holy in life.

Lent 2: The Gospel (Matt. 15. 21-28)

The story of the Canaanitish woman is probably one of the least attractive stories of the gospel. We like to think of our Lord's being always ready to help those who are in need. Instead, when the Canaanitish woman implored his help, "he did not answer her a word" (v. 23). Then again (for the woman was a Gentile): "I was sent only to the lost sheep of the house of Israel" (v. 24). Undaunted, she continues to implore his help. But there is even worse to come: "It is not fair to take the children's bread and throw it to the dogs" (v. 26). Not a very sympathetic portrait of the gracious Saviour!

The preacher's usual answer is to say that Jesus was out to test the woman's faith. Perhaps so; her refusal to be put off, her perserverance in asking in face of rebuttal is a remarkable demonstration of faith, that energetic grasping for the help of God. And it is her faith that Jesus praises at the end: "O woman, great is your faith!" (v. 28). All this is true enough as far as it goes. But there is more to it than that. The terms of Jesus' mission confined him to his own people. Even St Paul, that ardent missionary to the Gentiles, recognized this, for he writes that "Christ became a servant to the circumcised" (Rom. 15. 8). The Gospels agree with this. Jesus' public ministry was almost exclusively restricted to Jewish places—Capernaum, Nazareth, Bethsaida, Jerusalem. There was a purely Gentile city within a few miles from his native town, the then recently built city of Sepphoris, but it is never recorded that he ever went there. His contacts with Gentiles were strictly exceptional. In fact only three clear instances are recorded in the Gospels: the present pericope, the story of the centurion with the sick child or slave (Matt. 8. 5-13 = Luke 7. 1-10), and the episode of the Greeks at the feast (John 12. 20-26). This is remarkable, considering the battle that was fought in the later Church about the admission of Gentiles. Only three clear instances could be adduced to support their admission—incidentally a remarkable testimony to the basic honesty of our Gospels. Why was this? Did Jesus share the narrowness and exclusiveness of his people? Did he believe that salvation was, like some of the railway carriages in Nazi Germany, marked "For Jews only"? At first sight it certainly looks as though he did. But there is a saying where he speaks directly to this problem: "many will come from east and west and sit at table with Abraham, Isaac, and Jacob in the kingdom of heaven, while the sons of the kingdom will be thrown into the outer darkness" (Matt 8. 11f. par.). In other words, Jesus did accept the view that the Gentiles would be admitted finally, after the kingdom of God had come, but not before. Meanwhile, his ministry was directed particularly to the outcast among his own people: to the tax collectors, prostitutes, the riff-raff of society. Here we find that *in principle* the barrier between Jew and Gentile was indeed already broken down, for the barrier between them was the Law. If a man was to be saved it was not by his keeping of the Law, but simply by the forgiving grace of God. The gospel, then, was in principle not "for Jews only" on the basis of the works of the law, but for all who would accept it in faith, whether Jew or Gentile. Paul's theological arguments about this in Galatians and Romans merely draw out what was already implied in the conduct of Jesus in his earthly life: "For there is no distinction between Jew and Greek; the same Lord is Lord of all and bestows his riches upon all who call upon him" (Rom. 10. 12). But there is one crucial difference between the situation of Jesus and that of Paul. Paul stands on the other side of the death and resurrection of the Messiah. By his death and resurrection the kingdom of God has now been inaugurated. Now the many, the Gentiles, *can* come from the east and west and sit down with Abraham and Isaac and Jacob in the kingdom of God. Both Jesus and Paul took very seriously the barrier between Jew and Gentile. It was not lightly to be overcome. Overcome it would be, but only at the cost of death and resurrection of the Christ. Only his death could break down the barrier: "But now in Christ Jesus you who once were far off (i.e., the Gentiles) have been brought near in the blood of Christ. For he is our peace, who has made us both one, and has broken down the dividing wall of hostility, by abolishing in his flesh the law of commandments and ordinances, that he might create in himself one new man in place of the two, so making peace, and might reconcile us both to God in one body through the cross, thereby bringing the hostility to an end" (Eph. 2. 13-16). There *was* a barrier between Jew and Gentile. That barrier was the law. But the law, as a means of salvation, has been done away by the cross. Henceforth but only after the cross, can the Gentiles be admitted to the covenant. Similarly, the Christ of St John's Gospel says: "I, *when I am lifted up* from the earth (i.e., on the cross) will draw all men to myself" (John 12. 32). And at the Last Supper we are told that Jesus spoke of his blood as being shed for "many" (Mark 14. 24; cf. 10. 45). Modern scholars tell us that this "many" (like the saying about "many" from the east and the west) refers to the Gentiles.

The reluctance of Jesus to heal the daughter of the Canaanitish woman has to do with this theology about his death as the means of removing the barrier between Jew and Gentile. That barrier must be taken seriously. It is not simply that Jesus was out to test the woman's faith. The message of this pericope is that it is only through faith in the mercy of God in Christ—the mercy which is prefigured in this healing of the woman's daughter, but is not finally and decisively actualized until the cross—that the barrier is overcome and the Gentiles are admitted to salvation.

Thus, for all its unattractiveness—indeed, precisely in its unattractiveness—the gospel of Lent II proclaims an essential aspect of the doctrine of the cross. Through the cross the dividing wall between Jew and Gentile is broken down, the wall of the law regarded as the means of salvation. Our pericope is a proclamation of that "most wholesome Doctrine" which is "very full of comfort", that "we are justified by Faith only" (Article XI).

Lent 3 (Oculi): The Collect

Hidden away in this collect is a reminder of the basic purpose of this part of Lent (Lent I-IV), namely the sharing by all the faithful of the experience of the catechumens. For the "hearty desires" (Latin: *vota*, vows) "were the vows and decisions of the catechumens, who this week gave in their names to announce that they were ready to undertake the professions and responsibilities of Christian life".[7]

The goal towards which Lent moves is, or should be, quite concretely the renewal of our three baptismal vows, to renounce evil (as the epistles of Lent are teaching us), to believe (the proclamation of the saving act of God in Christ which is being expounded by the Lenten gospels), and to obey (as again the epistles are teaching us).

The phrase "from our enemies", though added by the Reformers, brings out the affinity between this collect and that of Lent II (see above pp. 43-45).

7 M. Shepherd, op. cit., pp. 128-129.

Lent 3: The Epistle (Eph. 5. 1-14)

This epistle belongs to the same series of instructions as the epistle of Lent II. Then the contrast between the old pagan life in which the converts to Christianity had previously lived, and the new life to which they were called in baptism, was defined in terms of the contrast between uncleanness and holiness. This week it is defined in terms of darkness and light (v. 8: "Once you were darkness, but now you are light in the Lord").

But before embarking upon this contrast between light and darkness, the author—whether Paul himself or (as many modern scholars think) a disciple of his—makes it quite clear that the standards of behaviour that he is about to demand are not based upon a legalistic ethic of what is "right" or "wrong"—words which are almost entirely absent from New Testament ethics—but upon the demand of love: "walk in love" (v. 2). By walking in love Christians are *imitating* God. The author does not scruple to speak of "imitation". Not of course that we can ever reproduce the same love as the love with which God loves. But Christian behaviour is meant to be a reflection of God's action towards us, specifically of his saving act in Christ: "as Christ loved us and gave himself up for us, a fragrant offering and sacrifice to God" (v. 2). There is no suggestion here of any distinction between Christ's love and God's love. There is no picture here of a loving Christ persuading an angry God to forgive. God's love and Christ's are one and the same thing: God's love is concretely manifested in Christ's offering of himself to God. God in Christ of his love undertook to do for us what he demanded of us but we could not do for ourselves, namely to offer a life of perfect obedience to him. This, however, is not in order to release us from the requirement of total obedience but to make that obedience possible in us for the first time. Hence the Christian life is a life of imitating the love which God actualized towards us in the incarnation and atonement.

Concretely, the life of love is to be exhibited—as in last week's epistle—in the sexual sphere. The concentration upon sexual behaviour is even more marked than the English translations suggest. Immorality, impurity, filthiness, silly talk, and levity

(i.e. bawdy talk) have an obvious sexual reference. But so too—
which is less obvious—have covetousness (vv. 3 and 5) and
idolatry (v. 5). Covetousness refers in this context explicitly to
coveting the neighbour's wife (as in the tenth commandment).
Idolatry likewise since the time of Hosea had been equated with
adultery (though here it is the other way round: adultery is
equated with idolatry). Originally this connection arose from
temple prostitution (see above). For us perhaps, the point is that
sexual licentiousness is equivalent to making sex a false god.

The author of Ephesians bluntly states (v. 5) that sexual sins
exclude the sinner from the kingdom of Christ and of God. This
may mean more than simply that people who do such things will
not go to heaven. It may mean that already the Church on earth
was exercising its power of the keys by excommunicating such
offenders, and that this action taken on earth was ratified in
heaven. The failure of our congregations today to exercise discipline over its members is part of the suburban captivity of the
Churches, part of the prevailing conformity to the world. For the
Reformers, especially Calvin, discipline was as essential to the life
of the Church as Word and sacraments.

That there have been grave misuses of the function of discipline
is undeniable. One need only think of the witch trials in New
England in the 1700s, or of the penalties inflicted on unfortunate
women in Scotland in respect of sexual offences during the same
period. The administration of discipline is a sore temptation to
those in authority to display an exaggerated self-righteousness, so
that they incur the Lord's condemnation. "Let him who is without
sin among you be the first to throw a stone at her" (John 8. 7).
But does that mean that *all* exercise of discipline should be
abandoned in the Church? A priest at his ordination is asked:
"Will you then give your faithful diligence always so to minister
the doctrine and sacraments, and *the discipline* of Christ . . .?"
Past abuses must not lead to the abandonment of one of the
essential activities of the Christian Church. On this matter the
main-line denominations have much to learn from, e.g., the
Mennonites.

The parallel warning of v. 6 ("Let no one deceive you with
empty words, for it is because of these things that the wrath of

God comes upon the sons of disobedience") has the same double reference—partly to ecclesiastical discipline and partly to the final judgement of God in the last day. It is a salutary warning today when there are so many, even within the Christian Church, who pass lightly over sexual immorality or suggest that it is a sign of progressiveness.

Lent 3: The Gospel (Luke 11. 14-28)

Like last week's gospel this pericope is also the story of an exorcism. As will be recalled from chapter 1 the catechumens in the ancient Church underwent a series of exorcisms (the driving out of the evil spirits) during their preparation for baptism. At Rome these exorcisms began on Lent 3. Hence this gospel had a very pertinent relevance when it was first chosen.

For us it is less obviously relevant. Demonic possession—at any rate in the western world—is no longer taken seriously. As we noted above (p. 41) even stories of exorcism brought home by missionaries fail to impress us. At best they may be psychologically explicable within a primitive culture. Yet the importance of this pericope for understanding our Lord's work can hardly be overestimated.

The exorcism itself is only briefly told. It simply serves to give occasion for a whole series of dominical sayings strung together to form a kind of sermon or discourse.

First of all comes the bystanders' reaction to the exorcism: "He casts out demons by Beelzebul" (Luke 11. 15). People often think it would be much easier to believe in Christ if we had seen him in the days of his flesh; if we had been there when he spoke with his tremendous authority, and performed his gracious deeds; if we had been there when they crucified him. Nothing could be further from the truth. The incarnation was not an immediately obvious thing. Rather, to hear Jesus' words and works was to be confronted by a decision with an either/or. Either it was through Beelzebul the prince of demons that he cast out demons (i.e., he was merely an ordinary human wonder-worker, trafficking in black magic), or it was by the finger of God (Matthew says "Spirit": the meaning is the same) that he cast them out. In choosing the way of incarnation to manifest himself and to perform the decisive act of our salvation God was taking a great risk. Here was no demonstrative proof, no "sign" (v. 16) from heaven, but a genuinely human life which could be explained either one way or the other. The whole life of Jesus is of a piece—his birth, his ministry, and above all his death on the cross. St Paul calls his death a "stumbling block" and "folly":

> For Jews demand signs and Greeks seek wisdom, but we preach Christ crucified, a stumbling block to Jews and folly to Gentiles, but to those who are called, both Jews and Greeks, Christ the power of God and the wisdom of God. For the foolishness of God is wiser than men, and the weakness of God is stronger than men (1 Cor. 1. 22-25).

Or again: "he was crucified in weakness" (2 Cor. 13. 4).

The incarnation and the cross hide as much as they reveal the presence of God. They are not *proofs*. The power of God in Jesus is perceptible only to the eyes of faith. When Peter makes his great confession: "You are the Christ, the Son of the living God", Jesus answers (according to Matthew): "Blessed are you, Simon Bar-Jona! For flesh and blood has not revealed this to you, but my Father who is in heaven" (Matt. 16. 16f.). A few years ago someone published a very silly book, a scroll purporting finally to disprove that Jesus was "divine". Such an idea is utter nonsense. Confronted by the words and works of Jesus, which culminate on the cross, you can either, if you are granted eyes to see and ears to hear, detect and confess the saving presence of God in him, or you may shut your eyes and stop your ears and say: "This man casts out demons by Beelzebul". So it was at the very beginning, and so it is today. It has to be a decision of faith, made by those who first "saw and believed", made today in response to the Church's preaching which passes on and brings alive again the testimony of those who first saw and believed.

Jesus never calls attention to himself, to his own status, his own "divinity" (such a word applied to Jesus is quite unbiblical). Rather, he calls attention to what God is doing in him: "If it is by the finger of God that I cast out demons, then the kingdom of God has come upon you" (v. 20). The decision of faith for which the Church calls is not capable of proof. But neither is it an arbitrary demand. For it is of a piece with the way Jesus himself understood his own word and work. He claimed that in him God was speaking and acting savingly (that is what is meant when he speaks of the kingdom or reign of God coming upon men through his words and works). Of course this is no proof that his claim is true. You could still say (however illogical that conclusion was, cf. vv. 17-19) that he was doing all this through Beelzebul. But it does mean that Jesus and the Church in its preaching after the resurrection are in the last resort of one mind about it. The Church has not arbitrarily imposed upon Jesus the idea that he in his word and work is the saving act of God. You cannot drive a wedge between Jesus and the Church in this matter, and say the Church got Jesus wrong, though even today popular writers still try this game, and often the man in the street is taken in. Either they (Jesus and the Church) are both wrong or they are both right. But that you have to decide. And what Jesus says about his exorcisms applies equally to the cross. For the cross was the culmination of that saving work which he began in his ministry, as he shows in another saying:

Behold, I cast out demons and perform cures today and tomorrow, and the third day I finish my course. Nevertheless I must go on my way today and tomorrow and the day following; for it cannot be that a prophet should perish away from Jerusalem (Luke 13. 32f.).

In the light of this last saying the gospel of Lent III has yet another bearing upon our misunderstanding of the cross. If the cross in the outcome of the Lord's entire saving ministry, it is the culmination of the battle between God and Satan. The "strong man" (Luke 11. 21) is Satan. The "one stronger than he" (v. 22) is Jesus as the agent of God's saving act. In the whole ministry, culminating in the cross, Satan is being assailed and overcome, the armour in which he trusted is being taken away, and his spoils are being divided. The cross, which looks so much like a defeat, is really victory. That means that Easter Day does not convert the defeat of Good Friday into a victory, but it manifests what Good Friday really means, namely, God's victory against Satan.

No doubt the rest of the sayings in this discourse had a special relevance for the catechumens. Verse 23 insists that there can be no neutrality in the conflict in which Jesus and Satan are engaged. Every man must choose his side. Verses 24-26 suggested to the catechumens that the exorcisms they are about to undergo are not merely negative. The evil spirits must be replaced by positive good, and for them that meant the Holy Spirit whom they were to receive when they were baptized.

For us, who are sharing in the liturgical experience of Lent, these verses are equally pertinent. Christians cannot be neutral in the conflict with Satan. And Lenten penitence is not enough: it must be followed by positive amendment.

Finally, the gospel of the day concludes with the incident of the woman who blurted out "Blessed is the womb that bore you, and the breasts that you sucked" (v. 27). She was flattering the preacher: "I enjoyed your sermon, Father!" How proud his mother must be to have such a fine preacher for a son! Jesus administers the woman a stern rebuke: "Blessed rather are those who hear the word of God and keep it!" (v. 28). The proper reaction to a sermon is to hear the word of God in it and to keep it. A good warning for Lent—whether the word we hear is in the sermon or in the liturgy. The eloquence of a sermon or the beauty of a liturgy must never intoxicate us into mere aesthetic enjoyment. There is no disparagement of Mary, the Mother of the Lord, in this text. After all, she *did* hear the word of God and kept it. And therefore all generations will call her blessed.

5

OASIS IN THE WILDERNESS
MID-LENT

Mid-Lent Sunday is like an oasis in the desert. But the fact that this is so is one of the accidents of history. In earlier times Lent actually began on the Monday after this Sunday. In those days as we have seen, Lent was much shorter. The third Sunday before Easter was originally the final fling of joy before the fasting began—a sort of early Mardi Gras or carnival. Then, when Lent was extended back another three weeks or more, this Sunday came to be in the middle. But it has always retained its more festive character. This is as it should be. All work and no play makes Jack a dull boy. We need bracing before the last lap, Passiontide, begins. That is sound psychology. But it is also sound theology. Unrelieved gloom is not Christian. Cheerfulness, as Dr Johnson was told, is always breaking in. Cheerfulness, however, not because of what we are but of what God has done. It is the gospel, the good news, that keeps breaking in even in the midst of our penitence. It is the glory of the resurrection that breaks into the gloom of the cross.

So we turn to the Propers for this Sunday,

THE FOURTH SUNDAY IN LENT
(LAETARE)

The ancient name of this Sunday, still current among Lutherans as well as Roman Catholics, though unfortunately largely (but by no means entirely) forgotten among Anglicans, is itself a constant

60

reminder of the more joyful character of this day. For it is the opening word of the antiphon of the Introit, "Rejoice!".

The Propers of this day have an interesting, though undesigned, history behind them. No one set out to select deliberately a series of texts which would speak of joy. What happened was this: Carrying on the note of joy and festivity inherited from the old days of the pre-Lenten carnival, the Bishop of Rome customarily distributed bread to the poor on this day—hence the feeding of the 5000 for the gospel. On this day, too, it was customary for the Pope to celebrate a "station mass". Instead of celebrating in his cathedral he went to one of the other churches in the city of Rome to celebrate. (This custom was dropped when the popes went into exile at Avignon, and has never been revived, though recently Popes John XXIII and Paul VI have begun to visit other churches in the city during the Sundays before Easter.) The station mass of this day was celebrated in the Basilica of the "Holy Cross in Jerusalem". Hence the epistle from Gal. 4. 21-5. 1a, with its mention of "Jerusalem above . . . our mother". The same purely fortuitous circumstance led to the selection of the passages for the Introit, the Gradual, and the Tract with the mention of Jerusalem (Introit), the Temple (Gradual), and Mount Sion (Tract). Despite the accidental character of these selections, they combine admirably to give a break in the penitential austerity of Lent. Even the instruction of the cate- chumens in the doctrines and ethical demands of the faith can be left temporarily aside. Thus a note of joy is struck in keeping with the earlier customs of this day.

Later on in the middle ages other customs grew up around this day. One was connected with the epistle and its reference to "Jerusalem, the mother of us all", and the pilgrim psalm (Ps. 122) used in the Introit and Gradual. In medieval England it was the custom for members of outlying congregations to make a pilgrim- age to the mother church of the diocese, and also, on the domestic level, for sons and daughters away from home to visit their parents. These customs gave this Sunday the name of "Mothering Sunday". The gospel likewise suggested the custom of baking a cake (according to a special recipe) called a "simnel" cake. The Sunday also acquired the name of "Refreshment Sunday" from the gospel. No other Sunday in the whole year has so many names nor so many customs attached to it.

Although the Book of Common Prayer has lost the Introit, this Sunday is so coloured by it that it calls for comment. The text reads (*English Hymnal* No. 679):

> (Antiphon) Rejoice ye with Jerusalem; and be ye glad for her, all ye that delight in her: exult and sing for joy with her, all ye that in sadness mourn for her; that ye may suck, and be satisfied with the breasts of her consolations.
>
> (Psalm verse) I was glad when they said unto me: We will go into the house of the Lord.

The antiphon is from Isa. 66. 10. It strikes a note of restrained joy, rather than the unbridled joy of Easter. The joy of Easter is the joy of sorrow turned into joy. Contrast the gospel of Easter 3 (*Jubilate*), with its parable of the woman in travail whose sorrow is turned into joy. This mid-Lent joy is a joy that breaks forth in the midst of sorrow. We are still in Lent, still mourning for Jerusalem, still in exile. But we look up and behold our redemption drawing nigh.

Lent 4: Collect

Only the collect fails to strike the exceptional note of this Sunday, of joy in the midst of sorrow. It is just one of the regular Lenten series of collects, very much like the others. Even the mention of "comfort" and "relief" in the petition really had nothing to do with "refreshment", though we may be tempted to read such a connection into it. It is simply a prayer for forgiveness, and comes from the penitential associations of Lent. We may take it as another reminder that the joy of *Laetare* is not the exuberant joy of Easter. We are still in Lent.

Lent 4: The Epistle (Gal. 4. 21-31 [and 5. 1a])

The Book of Common Prayer omits Gal. 5. 1a, an omission for which the English Reformers were unaccountably responsible. Earlier Roman and Lutheran usage, which included this verse, is better since it "gives a true climax to the theme of 'bondage versus freedom' ".[1] That indeed is the theme of the epistle. And although it had an entirely different origin from the earlier Lenten epistles it nevertheless forms a piece with them. For as earlier epistles had spoken of uncleanness *versus* purity (Lent II) and of darkness *versus* light (Lent 3), so this epistle speaks of bondage *versus* freedom. All these epistles thus prepare us for the *transitus* of Easter. But it also resounds with the peculiar joy of this Sunday, for freedom is the ground of the Christian's joy, the freedom of the Christian man of which Luther wrote, the freedom from the condemnation of the law.

Paul is writing to the Galatian Gentiles who are being tempted by false teachers to put themselves under the yoke of the law by becoming circumcised. He argues that this would be returning to the yoke of bondage, and casting away that freedom (for them a freedom from the "elements of the world" to which they were in bondage during their old pagan existence) wherewith Christ had set them free. He supports this argument by a scriptural proof from the story of Sarah and Hagar (Gen 16-17). This "proof" is singularly unconvincing to us, because it is based on an allegorical interpretation of the Old Testament alien to our way of thinking. For us scripture is meant to be taken literally. At best the Old Testament can only foreshadow the New by means of analogies. But Paul, whether he was following his early Rabbinic training or the kind of exegetical practice pursued at Qumran, allegorizes the story to produce the following complicated equation (set forth in the *Interpreters' Bible*, ad loc.):

Hagar = slavewoman = Sinai = law = flesh = Jerusalem "now" = mother of slaves.

Sarah = freewoman = promise = faith = Spirit = Jerusalem "above" = mother of freemen.

This allegory hardly convinces us today. But the case Paul is arguing is one of serious concern. We who are members of the Christian Church are free in Christ. It is vital that we understand what the freedom is and what it is not. Christian freedom is not to be confused with political liberty (though that may be a good thing worthy of the support of Christians). Christian

[1] M. Shepherd, op. cit., p. 130-131.

63

5

freedom is quite specifically freedom from the law, from the keeping of the law as the means of acquiring salvation by merit. But note that this does not mean that we are freed from the necessity of obedience. Since we are still sinful men, the law is still necessary to guide Christians into obedience—the so-called "third use of the law" of the Formula of Concord.[2]

The Christian has to walk on the razor's edge between legalism on the one hand and libertarianism on the other. And it is very difficult not to topple over one side or the other. All Christians need what is often called (somewhat dangerously perhaps) a "Rule of Life". In 1950 the Archbishops of Canterbury and York issued such a "rule", though they wisely called it "A Short Guide to the Duties of Church Membership". It reads as follows:

All baptized and confirmed members of the Church must play their full part in its life and witness. That you may fulfil this duty, we call upon you:

To follow the example of Christ in home and daily life, and to bear personal witness to him.

To be regular in private prayer day by day.

To read the Bible carefully.

To come to church every Sunday.

To receive Holy Communion faithfully and regularly.

To give personal service to Church, neighbours, and community.

To give money for the work of parish and diocese and for the work of the Church at home and overseas.

To uphold the standard of marriage entrusted by Christ to his Church.

To care that children are brought up to love and serve the Lord.

It is helpful and indeed necessary to have such a "rule of life". But we must understand and use it properly. It is intended for guidance—guidance for the fulfilment of the "law of Christ", the "law of liberty". It is not a means to secure our own salvation, but

[2] On this formula see above, p. 28.

64

an expression of gratitude for the fact that we have already been saved. The moment we understand it as "law" in the bad sense, the moment we think that by keeping such a rule we are putting ourselves right with God, then we must at once be warned, "For freedom Christ had set us free; stand fast therefore, and do not submit again to a yoke of slavery" (Gal. 5. 1).

Lent 4: The Gospel (John 6. 1-14)

We have already noted the purely fortuitous origin of this Sunday's gospel (above, p. 61). We might wonder why we should still retain it today, especially since the Feeding of the Multitude occurs on two or more Sundays in the Church year, (Trinity 7 in Mark's version, the Feeding of the Four Thousand; and on the Sunday next before Advent, again as on Lent 4 from St John).

The popularity of this lesson in the early Church was doubtless due to the fact that, quite rightly, it saw in the feeding of the multitude a foreshadowing of the eucharist. The author of the Fourth Gospel himself saw it in that light when he attached to it the discourse about the bread of heaven and about the eating and drinking of the flesh and blood of the Son of Man. But on each of the three Sundays when this story is used as a Sunday gospel it has a particular emphasis and setting. On the Seventh Sunday after Trinity, the season when the liturgy sets before us the ethical responsibilities of Christianity, it serves to remind us of our social responsibilities towards the "have-nots" of society: Jesus is reported as saying "I have compassion on the crowd, because they . . . have nothing to eat" (Mark 8. 2). On the Sunday before Advent it is read because by including v. 14 it expresses the theme of Christ's coming into the world: "This is indeed the prophet who is to come into the world!". It thus prepares us for Advent. What purpose does the same story of the feeding serve in Lent? Most obviously, it has given this Sunday the name "Refreshment Sunday". Lent is a kind of pilgrimage through the wilderness. The Gospel of Lent 1 had thrust us out into the wilderness with the children of Israel in their wanderings in Sinai, and with the Lord in his temptation. Now, on

Refreshment Sunday, the Lord feeds his people, as they wander through the wilderness, with the Bread of Heaven. To wander in the wilderness is not just a Lenten liturgical fancy. It says something about the whole Christian life. For just as the children of Israel wandered in the wilderness for forty years between the Exodus and their entry into the promised Land, so too the Church has a wilderness existence between Pentecost and Christ's second coming. This theme characterizes much of the New Testament, particularly the Epistle to the Hebrews, and also 1 Cor. 10. 1ff.:

> I want you to know, brethren, that our fathers were all under the cloud, and all passed through the sea, and all were baptized into Moses in the cloud and in the sea, and all ate the same supernatural food and all drank the same supernatural drink. For they drank from the supernatural Rock which followed them, and the Rock was Christ. Nevertheless with most of them God was not pleased; for they were overthrown in the wilderness.
> Now these things are warnings for us (1 Cor. 10. 1-6).

They are a warning for us because the Christian Church likewise is on a pilgrimage and in a wilderness situation. We exist between Pentecost and Christ's second coming, as the children of Israel existed in the wilderness of Sinai between their Exodus from Egypt and their entry into the promised land. As they embarked upon that pilgrimage in the cloud and through the sea, so the faithful embark upon the Christian pilgrimage through their baptism. As they were sustained with the water from the Rock and with manna, so Christians are sustained by the body and blood of Christ—"supernatural" food and drink—through the pilgrimage of the Christian life. The eucharist is in a true sense a *viaticum*, sustaining us as Elijah was sustained until he came to the mount of God.

But there is another reason why this gospel lesson is appropriate for this Sunday. Like all the other Lenten Gospels, it points towards the Passion. It is difficult to be sure what happened, historically speaking, at the feeding of the multitude.[3] But that something did happen cannot be doubted, however much the

[3] See the present writer's remarks in *Interpreting the Miracles*, (London, 1963), p. 37.

story has been subsequently written up in the light of the manna story and of Elijah's miraculous feeding of the hundred men with twenty loaves of barley (2 Kings 4. 42-44). The story is too well attested in so many strands of the tradition to dismiss it simply as the result of the legend-making activity of the early Church. But whatever actually did happen it undoubtedly was the occasion of a great crisis in our Lord's life. The Fourth Gospel gives the clue to this when it states that the crowd took him and wanted to make him king (John 6. 15). This explains Mark's curious note that after the feeding Jesus sent the disciples away while he dismissed the multitude (Mark 6. 45). Here, apparently, was the turning point in the ministry. Jesus' activity, culminating in the feeding, had aroused the expectations of the crowds to fever pitch. They completely misunderstood him and wanted to adopt him as the leader in a rebellion against Rome—like the Zealots. It was a crisis for Jesus. Either he would follow them, and thus abandon the path marked out for him at baptism and wrestled over in the temptations, or he must renounce their offer. He chose the latter path. As a result he parted company with the crowd, and concentrated on his closest disciples who were thus the remnants of a lost cause. He then prepares to take them up to Jerusalem, for a final challenge to the authorities, knowing full well that as a prophet he would perish at Jerusalem (Luke 13. 33). So there comes to us now at the critical turning point of Lent, just before the beginning of passiontide, the challenge, "Will you also go away?" (John 6. 67). Or will you, with the disciples, go up to Jerusalem in heart and mind during the coming passiontide, and follow him to the cross?

6

PASSIONTIDE

Modern revision of the Prayer Book marks off the last fortnight of Lent as "Passiontide" and the fifth Sunday in Lent as Passion Sunday. It has been claimed that the term, "Passiontide", was a nineteenth century Anglican invention.[1] But it is firmly embedded in Roman Catholic usage, as the *Catholic Encyclopedia* (1911) shows. The truth of the matter would seem to be that Anglicans only took it over from Roman Catholic usage in the nineteenth century. The term *Passionszeit* is not unknown to German Lutheranism, where it is often extended to mean the whole of Lent.

If the special name for this season is comparatively modern, the division of Lent at this point is much more ancient. Already in the middle ages in England it was customary to mark the distinctiveness of this part of Lent by changing the liturgical colour from Lenten white (unbleached linen) to passiontide red (a dull red mingled with black). Even modern Roman custom, so largely followed nowadays by Anglicans and American Protestantism generally, which uses violet throughout Lent, distinguishes Passiontide by the veiling of crosses, statues, and pictures from Passion Sunday on.

Yet despite these traditional distinctions, the difference between the two main parts of Lent is by no means clear cut. For one thing, the theme of the passion (it is, as we have suggested, the theme of penitence which is dominant on Ash Wednesday, and of baptismal instruction from Lent 1) is nevertheless already

[1] M. Shepherd, op. cit., p. 132 followed by Luther D. Reed, *The Lutheran Liturgy* (Philadelphia, 1947), p. 457.

present right from the beginning, as we have seen from the Old
Testament lessons and the gospels. Nor does the passion theme
fully take over until Palm Sunday. The propers for Passion
Sunday, as we shall see, still partake of the character of the earlier
Lenten Sundays, though the shadow of the cross, which had
already loomed over the preceding Sundays, now looms darker.
Here, in fact, is one of the most striking features of the Lenten
propers, the gradual accentuation of the cross, from the first
adumbrations of the passion to the temptations of Lent 1,
through the early conflicts with Satan in Lent 2 and 3, the turning
point of Lent 4 in the feeding of the 5000, and now on Lent 5 (as
we shall see) the sharpening of the issues of conflict between Jesus
and the Jews.

Passion Sunday (Judica): The Collect

It will be seen at a glance that there is nothing of the passion in
the collect of this day. It is of the same genre as the earlier Lenten
collects, a prayer for God's governance and preservation in body
and soul (cf. especially Lent 2). It is interesting to note that at
the projected revision of the Book of Common Prayer in 1689
the lack of the passion note led to the suggestion that the
traditional collect should be replaced by the following composition, based on the epistle of the day:

> O Almighty God, who hast sent thy Son Jesus Christ to be a
> High Priest of good things to come, and by his own blood to
> enter in once into the holy place, having obtained eternal
> redemption for us; mercifully look upon thy people, that by
> the same blood of our Saviour, who through the eternal Spirit
> offered himself without spot to thee, our consciences may be
> purged from dead works, to serve thee, the living God, that we
> may receive the promise of eternal heritance; through . . ..

Like so many post-Reformation Anglican collects, this is long-
winded and overloaded. Instead of the indirect allusiveness to
Scripture of the Latin collects it piles on phrases taken *verbatim*
from Scripture. We may well feel that the collect ought to strike
a note of the passion in harmony with the Scripture lesson. And

yet perhaps, our collect does contain one slight link with the passion. In the Latin Office hymn for Mattins at Passiontide, the last verse runs:

> To thee, eternal Three in One,
> Let homage meet by all be done:
> Whom by the Cross thou dost restore,
> *Preserve and govern* evermore.

(E.H. No. 94, italics mine)

The italicized phrase corresponds to the "govern and preserve us" in the collect. God's rule and governance, his guidance and preservation of his Church,[2] in his extension to it in the present of the benefits won by the passion of the Lord Jesus Christ.

Passion Sunday: The Epistle (Heb. 9. 11-15)

It is this epistle more than anything else which has given this Sunday the otherwise not too appropriate name "Passion Sunday". For here is "a classic statement of the theology of the passion"[3].

The Epistle to the Hebrews is a lengthy work, the central theme of which is a comparison between the sacrifices of the Old Covenant and the sacrifice of Christ. This central theme is developed in Heb. 7. 1-10. 18. In this central section today's liturgical epistle represents the absolute core of the argument, summing it up in a nutshell. So to read this extract is to get the gist of the whole argument of Hebrews. Only 10. 5-10, which will be read in the epistle on Good Friday, and which points up the obedience-character of Christ's sacrifice, adds anything really essential to what is stated here about it.

The author of Hebrews compares and contrasts the priesthood and sacrifice of the old covenant with the saving act of God in Christ. Both were initiated by God in order to bring men into communion and fellowship with himself in the activity of worship

[2] This is a prayer *for the Church*. In the BCP form, it opens with a prayer to God to look upon his "people"; in the original Latin the word translated "people" was "familia", family or household.

[3] *Liturgy and Worship*, ed. W. K. Lowther Clarke, (London, 1932), p. 391.

by removing the barrier to that communion, i.e. human sin. But the old covenant failed to achieve these things. It was impossible for animal sacrifices to take away sin. But what the old covenant could not achieve God in Christ has now effected. Christ is the high priest of *good things already come* (see R.S.V. at Heb. 9. 11). The good things which have already come are the blessings of the new age of salvation.: The scene in which the priest of the old covenant had carried out his high priestly work was the earthly tabernacle or tent in the wilderness. But this was only an earthly copy or shadow of the reality, namely the real presence of God himself. Christ however, carried out his high priestly work in a "greater and more prefect tent", in the reality itself, in the very presence of God, in the Holy Place, in heaven itself, in the real presence of God. At first sight this idea may seem a little strange. We have so long thought of sacrifice as consisting essentially in the killing of the victim, and have therefore tended to confine Christ's sacrifice to the moment of the cross, to Calvary. But a better understanding of sacrifice shows that it was a process. The slaying of the victim was no more than the essential preliminary to the supreme moment which was the presentation of the victim's blood—its offered-up life—to God. So in Christ's sacrifice the supreme moment is not simply what happened on the cross, but when the risen and ascended Christ presented his whole achievement, his sacrificed life, to the Father, and when the Father accepted it at the "moment" of the ascension. It is then that he entered in "once and for all"—in contrast to the priests of the Old Covenant who entered daily (or, in the case of the sacrifices of the Day of Atonement, yearly, but in either case repeatedly) into the earthly Holy Place. Moreover, his sacrifice consists not of something external to himself, not of the blood of calves and goats, not of some mere substitute for what God really requires (cf. 1 Sam. 15. 22f.; Hosea 6. 6; Micah 6. 6-8), but the offering of an obedient life. (This point is brought out more clearly, as we have seen, within the Good Friday epistle in Heb. 10. 5-10.) We must therefore not isolate Calvary from the whole of the incarnate life on the one hand any more than we must isolate it from the resurrection and ascension on the other. Calvary is the final outcome of a whole life of obedience.

71

The *effects* of the sacrifices of the old covenant and that of the new are then compared. The sacrifices of the old covenant could deal only with ritual offences, with inadvertent breaches of the ceremonial law. They could thus "sprinkle defiled persons", and serve to "the purification of the flesh", but they could do no more. Christ, however, obtained "an eternal redemption" for us. The effects of his sacrifice are not confined to a temporary removal of ritual impurities, but are eternal. That sacrifice removes once for all the real barrier between men and God—which is not inadvertent breaches of the ceremonial law, but sin. It "purifies our conscience from dead works" (i.e., from sin) to "serve the living God". The word "serve" (Greek *latreuein*) is primarily a liturgical word. The first effect of the eternal redemption Christ has achieved for us by his sacrifice is liturgical. It removes the barrier of communion between God and men, which sin is, and enables us to offer acceptable worship to God, "through Jesus Christ our Lord". But then of course liturgy issues in life, in obedient service. We can then go on to offer our whole lives as an acceptable sacrifice of obedience to God. "Do not neglect to do good and to share what you have, for such sacrifices are pleasing to God" (Heb. 13. 16).

Thus for all its emphasis on the once-for-all character of Christ's sacrifice, Hebrews does not mean that we are henceforth exempt from the obligation to offer and sacrifice ourselves. It means rather that we are now caught up into Christ's sacrifice—understood in the full sense in which we have expounded it—and offered by him to the Father in liturgy and in life.

Perhaps one of the boldest expositions of this has been given by a great nineteenth century Anglican preacher, F. W. Robertson of Brighton. His words are worth quoting in full:

> I say therefore that human life is a perpetual completion and repetition of the sacrifice of Christ—"all are dead"; the explanation of which follows, "to live not to themselves, but to him who died for them and rose again". This is the truth which lies at the bottom of the Romish doctrine of the Mass. Rome asserts that in the mass a true and proper sacrifice is offered up for the sins of all, that the offering of Christ is for ever repeated. To this Protestantism has objected vehemently, that there is but one

offering once offered, an objection in itself entirely true; yet the Romish doctrine contained a truth which it is of importance to disengage from the gross and material form with which it has been overlaid. Let us hear St Paul: "I fill up that which is behindhand of the sufferings of Christ, in my flesh, for his body's sake, which is the Church". Was there, then, something behindhand of Christ's sufferings remaining uncompleted, of which the sufferings of Paul could in any sense be the complement? He says there was. Could the sufferings of Paul for the Church in any form of correct expression be said to eke out the sufferings that were complete? In one sense it is true to say that there is one offering once offered for all. But it is equally true to say that one offering is valueless, except so far as it is completed and repeated in the life and self-offering of all. This is the Christian's sacrifice. Not mechanically completed in the miserable materialism of the mass, but spiritually in the life of all in whom the crucified lives. The sacrifice of Christ is done over again in every life which is lived not to self but to God.[4]

What the epistle for Passion Sunday affirms in its concluding verse and what Robertson is trying to say here are one and the same thing. The doctrine of atonement through Christ's sacrifice does not mean that we are released from the necessity of obedience, but that we are freed precisely for obedience.

Two illustrations may show how, although the atonement wrought in Christ is in the first instance vicarious (in the sense that he does for us what we are incapable of doing for ourselves), nevertheless we are then caught up into it and enabled to do what we could not do before. The first is from the late C. S. Lewis. When a child is learning to write but is as yet unable to form the letters with his own hand, a kindly parent encloses the child's small hand in his own big one and traces the letters: the child is thus enabled to make the letters. So we can offer the sacrifice of ourselves in Christ.

The second comes from Dr Eduard Schweizer, the Swiss New Testament scholar. When a Swiss child living up in the Alps has to go to school the day after a heavy snow fall, too deep for him to walk by himself, his father will walk ahead and blaze

[4] F. W. Robertson, *Sermons on Christian Doctrine*, (Everyman Edition, London and New York, n.d.), pp. 95f.

the trail in front of him. So the child can walk in the father's footsteps. It would have been no good if the father had simply gone to the school himself. The son must follow. Yet he could not have gone alone. In the first instance the father was doing what the child could not do for himself. But it is more than an example for the son to copy. The father's prior action has power which enables the son to do what he could not do for himself.

Passion Sunday: The Gospel (John 8. 46-59)

This is an extract from one of the great dialogues of the Fourth Gospel, the christological dialogue (i.e. concerned with the doctrine of Christ's person). To some it will seem perfectly natural that Jesus should have spoken to his adversaries in this way. It is in the Bible and therefore occasions no difficulties. To others it will seem abhorrent that he should ever have spoken so. To them it will seem wholly inconsistent with the teaching of the Sermon on the Mount and an example of the incipient anti-Semitism of Christianity. Such people will welcome the relief afforded by modern scholarship, which attributes the dialogues and discourses of the Fourth Gospel to the Fourth Evangelist rather than to Jesus himself.

It is true that the dialogues of the Fourth Gospel are, as they stand, the compositions of the Fourth Evangelist. We cannot normally go to them in order to establish the words which Jesus actually spoke. For instance (and this is very important) we cannot infer from the great climactic statement at the end of today's gospel "Before Abraham was, I am", that Jesus himself explicitly affirmed his own pre-existence. Any modern study of New Testament Christology makes it clear that the pre-existence of Christ was an affirmation that was not made until the Christian gospel was taken to the Greek-speaking world. This christological doctrine seems to have originated earlier than St Paul though it has sometimes been attributed to him. It seems also to have been based on the identification of Christ with the Wisdom of God. In Hellenistic Jewish thought wisdom was more or less personified and regarded as the pre-existent agent of creation, and of continuing revelation to and inspiration of holy men. This identification of Jesus with the heavenly wisdom of God may seem a long cry from the earliest Christology, which proclaimed him as the Son of man who was to return as Judge and Saviour at the end (Acts 3. 20f.) and from the slightly later Christology which identified him with the Christ and Lord who was now exalted and reigning in the heavens (Acts 2. 36). Still more does it seem a far cry from Jesus' own historical self-understanding as the one whose word and work confronted men and women with the saving presence and action of God himself. But it is not so really. All Christology means that Jesus is the one in whom God was present and acting savingly, both in his earthly history and in the continuation of his word and work in the preaching and sacraments of the Christian community. God *was* in Christ and *is* in Christ. All this means that the God who was present in him, going forth in saving action, is the same God who created the heavens and the earth. He is the same God who went out of himself in revealing action in the creation and preservation of the universe, and in the revelation of himself in the history of men, particularly in the history of Israel. The Word or Wisdom of God is God going out of himself in revealing action, in creation and redemption. When St John makes the earthly Jesus say, "Before Abraham was, I am", he is really only making explicit what was implicit in Jesus' own proclamation, in his own word and work, in the preaching of the earlier community.

But there is more in the discourses of the Fourth Gospel than a formulation of the theology of the latest Christian community of New Testament times. Those discourses revolve around earlier, traditional sayings of Jesus, they meditate upon them and draw out their deepest implications. So it is in the passage appointed for the gospel on Passion Sunday. It touches earlier tradition at many points and enshrines earlier sayings. The Jews' charge that Jesus had a demon (v 48) echoes the charge in the Synoptic Gospels (which figured in the gospel of Lent 3), that he was in league with Beelzebul, the prince of the devils. There Jesus had claimed that it was by the finger of God that he was performing his exorcisms. He was thereby claiming that his works were indeed the present, direct action of God himself. His exorcisms in the synoptic tradition are of a piece with and part of his word, the proclamation of the present Reign of God: "The kingdom of God has come upon you". All this is here translated into Johannine language. "I honour my Father" (v.49). Even the name "Father", Abba, is typical of Jesus' own manner of speech in the Synoptic Gospels. "If any man keeps my word, he will never see death" (v. 52). So too, in the earlier tradition, Jesus challenges men to accept his word now, so that they may be accepted into salvation at the End: "Every one who acknowledges me before men, the Son of man also will acknowledge before the angels of God; but he who denies me before men will be denied before the angels of God" (Luke 12. 8f.). Or again, as the parables of the lost sheep (Luke 15. 3–7) and the lost coin (Luke 15. 8–10) assert, Jesus by eating and drinking with publicans and sinners is the agent of God's seeking and saving the lost, so that there is joy in the presence of the angels of God over one sinner who repents. The Johannine Christ makes the same point here, in different language, when he says, "If any one keeps my word, he will never taste death" (John 8. 52). Jesus' word, his message, his proclamation is God's ultimate offer of salvation, which will be ratified at the End.

Where does Abraham come into all this? Here again, the Fourth Evangelist is in contact with the earlier tradition. For John the Baptist had likewise warned the Jews not to be complacent about their descent from Abraham. God was able of the very stones to raise up children to Abraham! (Matt. 3. 9 par). Salvation depended on a response to the word of God, not upon physical descent. St Paul took up the same line of thought in his letters to the Galatians and the Romans (Gal. 3—4; Romans 4). This penetrates to the heart of the issue between Jesus and his adversaries, as it is already presented in the synoptic tradition. That is why so many people refused to accept his offer of salvation—just as they continued to reject the offer of that salvation in the preaching of the apostles after the resurrection. They were deluded by a false sense of security. Secondly, there is the staggering claim, "Abraham rejoiced that he was to see my day; he saw it and was glad" (v.56). Abraham in his lifetime foresaw the advent of the Messianic salvation. It is difficult to pinpoint precisely what passage of scripture in Genesis the Evangelist had in mind. Most probably he was thinking of a Rabbinic interpretation of the statement in Gen. 24. 1 that Abraham was "well advanced in years". According to Rabbinic interpretation this meant that Abraham was granted a vision of all the days to come (the Hebrew here could be translated literally to say "Abraham was gone into days") *including the day of the Messiah*. Alternatively, the statement that "Abraham was glad" may be an interpretation of his joy at the birth of Isaac (Gen. 17. 17), who was a type of the Messiah. However precisely we explain the allusion, it clearly means that somewhere along the line Abraham greeted the Messianic salvation from afar. And the Messianic salvation was precisely what the Jesus of history offered men and women in his word and work. And it was precisely their rejection of that salvation that was involved in the plot of the Jewish authorities to get rid of Jesus. Thus does this discourse penetrate to the heart of the issue between Jesus and Israel which led him to the cross. Although couched in terms of high Johannine theology, it correctly interprets the actual history of Jesus.

PALM SUNDAY

The popular name of this Sunday is certainly very ancient and indeed goes back to the enterprise of Bishop Cyril of Jerusalem (see above p. 20). The triumphal entry is really only a secondary theme of the day. In the Latin liturgy, the reading of the Palm Sunday story and the procession of the palms belongs not to the Mass itself, but to a preliminary service. Only recently, in some modern Anglican revisions of the Prayer Book, has the Palm Sunday story gained a foothold in the liturgy itself. It has not fully succeeded in the Prayer Book of the Protestant Episcopal Church in the U.S.A., though St Mark's Palm Sunday story (Mark 11. 1-11) is there provided as second lesson at Morning Prayer. We shall not, however, wish to suppress the Palm Sunday theme altogether, for it forms a magnificent introduction to the

77

contemplation of the passion during this week. It displays the paradoxical royal dignity of him who goes to the cross:

> Tell the daughter of Zion,
> Behold, *your king* is coming to you,
> humble, and mounted on an ass,
> and on a colt, the foal of an ass.
>
> (Matt. 21. 5, cf. Zech. 9. 9)

(The hymn "Ride on! ride on in majesty!" (EH 620, esp. vv 2 and 5) is full of the paradox.) Quite fittingly, this is under-lined by an Old Testament lesson appointed for optional use at the Holy Communion, Zech. 9. 9–12. In the American Prayer Book, the lectionary appoints this passage for Morning Prayer, and in the new (American) *Liturgy of the Lord's Supper* it may as in England be used as an Old Testament lesson in the liturgy. In it, again, the Church joins the Palm Sunday crowds with the welcome: "Hosanna to the Son of David! Blessed is he who comes in the name of the Lord! Hosanna in the highest!" "In the light of Christian faith the misunderstanding of the crowds is redressed, and the Church welcomes the Christ advancing to die for the salvation of the world".[5] For the crowds misunderstood him as a political, earthly king.

The rest of the Palm Sunday propers quite rightly concentrate on the passion itself. All of Holy Week is really an extended Good Friday, itself originally part of the ancient paschal festival which celebrated both the death and the resurrection of Christ. Holy Week and Easter Day have to be lived through as a total liturgical experience, as a participation in the transition of Christ passing through death to resurrection.

Palm Sunday: The Collect

The poignant phrase "of thy tender love" was added to this collect by Cranmer. The love of God is not just benevolent sentiment of a general kind, but a concrete event. That event embraces both the incarnation ("take upon him our flesh") and the cross. Catholics have tended to isolate the incarnation from the atonement and to build upon it some general incarnational

[5] E. C. Hoskyns and F. N. Davey, *The Fourth Gospel* (London, 1940), p. 494.

philosophy. Protestants have tended to isolate the atonement from the incarnation, and to put a wedge between God and Christ. This collect, like today's epistle and like Luther's sermons, forbids us to isolate incarnation and atonement in this way. Both form a single, indivisible movement of the love of God, a supreme act of condescension. Although no one could accuse this collect of teaching a purely exemplarist doctrine of the atonement (in view of its assertion that incarnation and passion are the supreme act of the saving love of God), yet the passion—and the idea is taken from the epistle of the day—is *also* treated as an example of humility and patience. But to follow the example of Christ's passion is not to copy or imitate the external example. It is to allow the grace of God to conform us to the passion and so produce in us the fruits of humility and patience. And it is through this that we shall "be made" partakers of his resurrection. This is no reward for merit, but an act of pure grace. It is God's act conforming us to the passion of his Son. This indeed is the whole purpose of our reliving of the passion and resurrection in the liturgy of Holy Week and Easter.

Palm Sunday: The Epistle (Phil. 2. 5–11)

It is generally agreed among scholars today that St Paul is here quoting from an early Christian hymn. Since the language of the hymn is markedly different from his own, it was probably composed by someone prior to the apostle himself. When we come to reconstruct the hymn, however, we are faced with a number of different proposals, and there is no general agreement about the most likely form. Here is a recent proposal which has much to commend it:[6]

1

Who, though he was in the form of God,
did not count equality with God a thing to be grasped,
but emptied himself,
taking the form of a servant.

6 Charles H. Talbert, *JBL* 86 (1967), pp. 141-153. My own interpretation of the hymn is however very different from the one offered in that article.

2

Being born in the likeness of men
and being found in human form he humbled himself
and became obedient unto death.[7]

3

Therefore God has highly exalted him
and bestowed on him the name
which is above every name,

4

that at the name of Jesus
every knee should bow, in heaven and on earth
and under the earth,
and every tongue confess "Jesus Christ is Lord"
to the glory of God the Father.

The exact interpretation of almost every phrase is very much in dispute among scholars. What follows is, in the view of the present writer, the most likely interpretation.

Stanza 1 alludes briefly to the pre-existence of the Redeemer. As the divine wisdom he was "in the form of God". That is to say, he enjoyed a divine mode of existence, the state of "equality with God" (line 2). The same stanza (lines 2 and 3) then goes on to speak of his becoming incarnate. He did not hold on to the divine mode of existence, but voluntarily surrendered it, and took upon himself the mode of human existence. The human mode of existence is characterized as that of a servant, or better, of a slave. The word "slave" indicates that the stanza is not speaking of what is unique about the incarnate One, (e.g., that he is the "Servant of God" as in Isa. 53), but of what he shares in common with all other men. This slavery is bondage to the powers of evil—particularly of sin and death. It is the same point that comes to focus in the cry from the cross, "My God, my God, why hast thou forsaken me?"

Stanza 2 speaks of the incarnate life of the Redeemer, contrasting that life with the life of Adam, the first man. Adam

[7] It is generally agreed that the words "even death on a cross" disturb the poetic rhythm and were a footnote added by St Paul to the original hymn.

80

lifted himself up in pride and disobeyed. The Christ humbled himself and became obedient to the will of God, amid man's state of bondage which had been incurred by the first man's disobedience. Thus the Christ reverses man's bondage.

Stanza 3 sets the seal to this obedience. God vindicates him ("wherefore": Christ's resurrection is consequent upon his obedience to death). God exalts him "more highly". Not indeed more highly than the mode of existence he had enjoyed in his preexistence state—for nothing could have been higher than equality with God—but more highly than all the powers of evil which had held man in bondage. This divine mode of existence is, however, superior in one thing—it is now a "name", identifiable, manifest, revealed to the powers as victorious over them.

Stanza 4 looks forward to this final consummation when the powers acknowledge their defeat and the Lordship of Christ will be universally confessed.

There are highly mythological elements in this hymn. There is the wisdom speculation, the idea of wisdom's descent into the world. There is the idea of the powers which hold men in bondage, and of their subjugation over them. But these mythological elements are placed at the service of concrete historical facts—the human reality of the Redeemer, and his obedience even to death. And there is also behind it a real experience of the early Christian community. This is the experience of the difference which the cross of Christ has made to human existence. Through the cross man is liberated from his old existence under sin and death which are his ultimate separation from God. That is the experience to which the hymn gives expression. It has mythological elements in it but it is not mere "mythology".

As a reading for Palm Sunday this epistle is singularly appropriate. It prevents us from isolating (as so much Christian theology and devotion has done) the cross from the incarnation and the earthly ministry of Jesus on the one hand, and from his exaltation and the final consummation on the other. The cross is viewed as the culmination of the humiliation of the Son of God, and at the same time (note the "wherefore" at the beginning of stanza 3) as the ground and cause of his triumph. In short, it speaks of both humiliation and triumph, the very same themes which are expressed in the Palm Sunday story of the triumphal entry. The epistle serves as a bridge between the subsidiary theme of the day, the triumphal entry, and the Passion according to St Matthew, which is to follow.

THE HOLY WEEK EPISTLES
MONDAY, TUESDAY, WEDNESDAY

Monday before Easter: Epistle (Isaiah 63. 1-19)

The pre-Reformation use of Sarum had Isaiah 50. 5–10 as the epistle of this day, just like the Roman rite. For some unknown reason, the first English Prayer Book (1549) shifted Isaiah 50 to Tuesday, and got its new Monday epistle from the Sarum provision for Wednesday in Holy Week, but lengthening it to cover the whole chapter.

This lesson falls into two halves:
1. Verses 1–6. A double dialogue between the Prophet and Yahweh.
2. Verses 7–19 (and on through v. 12 in Chapter 64). The prophet's prayer for Israel

Section (2) is subdivided thus:
(a) Verses 7–9: a recitation of Yahweh's mighty acts in Israel's history.
(b) Verses 10–14: a confession of Israel's unfaithfulness throughout her history.
(c) Verses 15–19: an intercession for Israel—a petition for her restoration.

Thus the prayer follows the normal pattern of biblical prayer: a rehearsal of God's mighty acts, followed by a confession of past sin, and thence to intercession and petition. The original context of this passage was probably the period after the return from the Babylonian exile (Sixth Century B.C.). By now it was clear that the return was not the splendid event that the Second Isaiah (chapters 40–55) had predicted. The rebuilding of the temple and of the city had turned out to be a "stop-go" affair. This prayer arises from the ensuing disillusionment.

What has it to do with Holy Week and the passion? Strictly speaking, very little. One might have preferred for these three days a series of Old Testament lessons from the four Servant songs of Second Isaiah (Isaiah 42. 1-4; 49. 1-6; 50. 4-9; 52. 13-53. 12). Only one of these is used, namely, on Tuesday (see below). It is possible, with a little ingenuity, to find some relevance to the passion in the first section of our lesson. Here Yahweh is pictured as a blood-spattered warrior coming home from battle with Edom (one of Israel's traditional enemies). A rather repulsive picture! The prophet asks who this victorious warrior is (verses 1a and b). In verse 1c comes the response "It is I"—the characteristic self-designation of Yahweh which the Fourth Gospel puts onto the lips of Jesus. Yahweh speaks "in righteousness" ("announces vindication", RSV). His victory over his enemies is a mighty act of salvation for Israel.

The second question of the prophet is Why?—why are the warrior's garments sprinkled with blood like a worker in the wine press stained with the blood of the grape? The answer is: he has been fighting the battle single-handed, and is drenched in the blood of his enemies (verses 3-6): "*their* lifeblood was sprinkled upon my garments . . . I poured out *their* lifeblood on the earth". A powerful picture, but not very Christian, and hardly suitable as it stands as an interpretation of Jesus' passion. The Book of Revelation has however given this passage a Christian reinterpretation, and this Christian reinterpretation of our passage can alone justify its use in Holy Week: [8]

> So the angel swung his sickle on the earth and gathered the vintage of the earth, and threw it into the great winepress of the wrath of God; and the winepress was trodden outside the city, and blood flowed from the winepress (Rev. 14. 19f.).

> Then I saw the heaven opened, and behold a white horse! He who sat upon it . . . is clad in a robe dipped in blood, and the name by which he is called is the Word of God . . . he will tread the winepress of the fury of the wrath of God (Rev. 19. 11ff.).

In the first quotation the phrase "outside the city" suggests that the event referred to in symbolic language is the crucifixion (cf. Heb. 13. 13; Matt. 21. 39). In the second quotation "Word of God" is a title for Jesus Christ. Again, in the second quotation the blood in which the garment worn by the Christ is dipped is

[8] Cf. A. T. Hanson, *The Wrath of the Lamb* (London, 1957) p. 16: "We may in fact say that these two pictures from "Trito-Isaiah" [i.e., Isaiah 59. 17f and our passage] are what the divine wrath would look like if you imagine a divine intervention in history without the Cross."

best understood as his own blood, shed upon the cross. And, as the reference in both passages to the winepress of God's wrath shows, it is the picture of Isaiah 63 that the seer has before him.

Viewed in this way, the Isaiah prophecy fits surprisingly with the passion according to St Mark, the beginning of which it accompanies on this day. "I have trodden the winepress alone . . .. I looked, but there was no one to help. I was appalled, but there was no one to uphold" (vv. 3 and 5). It is St Mark, as we shall see, who among the Evangelists stresses the loneliness of Christ in his passion, as he grapples in single-handed combat with the foe. The foe is of course no longer Edom or Israel's other enemies, but the prince of darkness and his minions. And it is St Mark, too, who in the sole word that he records from the cross deliberately portrays Christ as standing in our place and enduring God's wrath upon sin.

The ensuing prayer, with its recitation of Israel's salvation history and the confession of Israel's rebellion throughout that history, is even less directly linked to the passion. Yet in the perspective of the Gospels and of the New Testament as a whole[9] the exordium of the prophet's prayer recites a salvation history of which the Christ event is the climax.

There are some points of detail in the prophet's prayer which merit closer inspection. In verse 9 we read: "In all their affliction he was afflicted". Yahweh is not a distant uninvolved God, but one who identified himself unreservedly with his people in their affliction. The prophet discerned this pattern of divine action already in Israel's history. It began at the Exodus: "I have seen the affliction [N.B. the Hebrew word for affliction here is different from that in Isaiah 63. 9, so we cannot be sure that the prophet definitely had this particular passage in mind], and I have come down to save them" (Exod. 3. 7). The involvement of Yahweh with his people reaches its climax in the perspective of Christian faith, in the incarnation and passion of Jesus.

In the second part of the prayer, the confession of Israel's sins, there are two remarkable Old Testament references to God's "holy Spirit" (vv. 10, 11, cf. also v. 14). It is perhaps surprising that so little attention has been paid to these passages as a background

[9] Cf. the parable of the Wicked Husbandmen, Mark 12. 1-9.

for the New Testament concept of the Holy Spirit. The source of this concept is normally seen, and rightly enough, in the later hope of Israel for a great outpouring of the Holy Spirit in the last days (cf. the prophecy in Joel 2. 28 and various prophecies in Second Isaiah, Jeremiah, and Ezekiel). This expectation was certainly very much alive in the Jewish piety of our Lord's day—to some extent in the apocalyptic writings, but more so in the rabbinic tradition. That the Spirit of Yahweh was operative in the Old Testament period in the great figures of Israel's history, especially in Moses and the prophets, has been generally recognized, and it is here very largely the origin of the expectation of a great outpouring of the Spirit in the last days has been sought. But our passage (Isaiah 63. 10ff.) opens up broader possibilities. It was an accepted dogma of late Judaism that the events of the Exodus would be repeated at the End. Thus, there was to be a fresh Exodus out of Egypt, a fresh crossing of the Red Sea, a repetition of the miracles of the cloud, the manna, and the water from the rock. These ideas St Paul takes up in 1 Cor. 10 and sees their fulfillment in the Christian dispensation. Our passage suggests that the expectation of the outpouring of the Spirit in the last days likewise originates from this same complex of ideas. According to our passage the Holy Spirit of Yahweh was especially present in Israel's salvation history from the Exodus on. For it was precisely at the Exodus, according to vv. 11f., that Yahweh put his Holy Spirit in the midst of his people. This same phenomenon is therefore expected at the end, and is fulfilled after the death and resurrection of Jesus, the Christian Exodus, as a result of which the Holy Spirit is finally poured upon the new people of God in the last days. That the early Christians were aware of our passage is perhaps indicated by the echo of verse 10 in Eph. 4. 30. But again we cannot be quite sure, since the word for "grieve" in the Ephesians passage is different from the word used in the Greek translation of Isaiah 63. 10. From these considerations an important conclusion emerges. The Holy Spirit is a concept of salvation history. In both the Old Testament and the New the presence of the Spirit is the outcome of the primary redemptive act of God (Exodus in the Old Testament and cross-resurrection in the New Testament). And in both Old

Testament and New it is the Holy Spirit's function to continue in the ongoing life of the people of God the salvation history which has been inaugurated by the primary redemptive event.

Finally, there is the twofold affirmation of faith in the fatherhood of God in Isaiah 63. 16. It is sometimes said that the fatherhood of God is one of the distinguishing articles of Christian faith as contrasted with the Old Testament and Judaism. This is quite unfair to the latter. True, the concept of God as Father is not prominent in the Old Testament. True, too, there is a difference between the Old Testament-Jewish conception of the divine fatherhood and that of Christian faith. For the Christian knows himself to be admitted to the privilege of addressing God as Father through Christ alone (Luke 11. 2 RSV; Gal. 4. 6; Rom. 8. 15), who addressed God as "Abba", the intimate address of the Jewish child to his earthly father.[10] The shape of the concept is the same in both Testaments; the Fatherhood of God is not a universal, natural truth which every man can apprehend for himself, just as men are not by nature the sons of God. Knowledge of the divine fatherhood depends in both Testaments upon the redemptive event in which God is disclosed to his covenant people. In the Old Testament that event is the Exodus, and in the New it is the incarnation, cross, and resurrection of Jesus Christ. Thus the first disclosure of the divine Fatherhood of which our lesson speaks sets the pattern for the second disclosure, which we celebrate at passiontide and Easter.

Tuesday before Easter: Epistle (Isaiah 50. 5-11)

This is as we have seen the old pre-Reformation lesson for Monday in Holy Week. Formerly it ended at verse 10, a better ending for the lesson. For verses 4-9 represent the third of the four servant songs of second Isaiah (see above p. 83). Verses 10-11 do not belong to the song but from the climax of chapters 49-50. So we shall confine our attention to verses 4-9.

In this song the unknown prophet pictures himself as Yahweh's servant. He receives his prophetic message from God:

10 See Joachim Jeremias, *The Central Message of the New Testament* (New York, 1965), pp. 9-30.

"The Lord God has given me the tongue of those who are taught" (v. 9). Each day the prophet receives from Yahweh the word which he is to pass on to God's people: "Morning by morning he wakens, he wakens my ear to hear . . . the Lord has opened my ear" (verses 4-5). The people of Israel are "weary" (verse 4). It is not clear from the context whether they are weary with their prolonged exile in Babylon, or weary from constantly having the word of God dinned into their ears by the prophet. The latter meaning would certainly prepare the way for verse 6: the smiters and those who pull out the prophet's beard, put him to shame, and spit on him are the people of Israel who reject the prophet's word (the sufferings of the prophet are probably modelled on those of Jeremiah). But the prophet gives himself undeterred to his mission: he is not rebellious, he does not turn back. He sets his face like a flint, confident that Yahweh will vindicate him in the end (verses 7-9).

This song is eminently applicable to Jesus' passion, and perhaps the New Testament itself is aware of this. At first sight the picture of the servant as the recipient of a word from Yahweh to pass on to Israel may seem inapplicable to Jesus, who confronts Israel as the independent source of his message (*"I* say unto you", rather than "Thus saith the Lord"). Yet the Fourth Gospel, which probes much more deeply into the inner relations between Jesus and his Father than does the synoptic tradition, affirms: "He bears witness to what he has seen and heard . . . for he whom God has sent utters the words of God" (John 3. 32). The Fourth Gospel is here talking on two different levels: on one level it is speaking of the historical Jesus. In his baptism (cf. John 3. 34, which speaks of Jesus receiving the plenitude of the Spirit, and the reference to his "sealing" by God in John 6. 27) Jesus receives from the Father the message of the inbreaking of the final kingdom of God which he is to declare to Israel. But on another level, this kind of language speaks of the eternal relationship between the Father and the Son.[11] It is precisely in this dynamic relationship that the inner-trinitarian relations of the Father and the Son are disclosed in history. Now all this looks like the speculation of

[11] See F. Gogarten, *Demythologizing and History* (London, 1955), pp. 72f.

the Fourth Gospel and seems to have little root in the historical Jesus himself. It is however exactly what is implied by Jesus' use of "Amen" in his constantly repeated declaration "Amen (AV 'verily') I say unto you". The striking point about this turn of phrase is that Judaism, like later Christianity, commonly used Amen at the end of prayers, rather than at the beginning of declarations. Used at the end of a prayer, Amen expresses the faith that God will answer the prayer—a faith which is nevertheless a hesitant aspiration rather than a confident assertion: "Lord, I believe, help thou mine unbelief". With Jesus, however, it is different. Jesus dares to preface his declarations (not his aspirations) with the confident claim that what he is about to say is the absolute truth of God himself. This because, as Gerhard Ebeling has pointed out, Jesus had made himself (in his baptism?) a prior ultimate commitment of faith to his Father, so aligning his words with the Father's word, which he can now pass on to others. This too, is the New Testament justification for the new doctrine of Christ's person (Christology) which Bishop Robinson has sketched out as a programme in *Honest to God*—Christ as the one man who has so opened himself to the ground of Being that he becomes for us a window into the Being of God.[12]

To return to the servant song of Isaiah 50, there are some slight suggestions that this song was one of the models for the description of Jesus' passion in the Gospels. While there is no direct verbal parallel, as might have been expected, with the description of Jesus' scourging by Pilate in Mark 15. 15, the word for "blows" is exactly the same word as occurs in the Greek version of Isaiah 50. 6, which reads "they gave my cheeks to *blows*." Matthew, taking up Mark's hint, has deliberately underlined the echo of Isaiah 50. 6, for he rewords Mark thus:

Isaiah 50.6	*Mark 14.65*	*Matthew 26. 67*
I hid not my *face* from shame and *spitting*	And some began to *spit* on him, and to cover his *face*	Then they *spat on his face*

Here is the New Testament justification for reading this passage

[12] J. A. T. Robinson, op. cit. (London, 1963), pp. 70-5.

on Tuesday in Holy Week as a description of the Lord's own passion.

The second part of the song (verses 7–9) speaks of the servant's ultimate vindication by Yahweh after delivering his word and being rejected and shamefully treated: "He who vindicates [AV 'justifieth', a more literal rendering of the Hebrew] me is near." This theme of vindication recalls the terms in which the earliest Church preached the resurrection of Jesus. It would seem that before a theology of atonement was formulated (Mark 10. 45, 14. 24),[13] Jesus' death and resurrection were interpreted in terms of Ps. 118. 22 ("The stone which the builders rejected has become the headstone of the corner"), as God's Yes (vindication) in response to Israel's No. By going up to Jerusalem Jesus had staked all on the truth of his message, "The Kingdom of God has drawn near." He set his face "like a flint" (see Luke 13. 32–33). Israel, in the person of her religious rulers, rejected this message, thereby apparently discrediting it for ever. But, the Christians proclaimed, God raised Jesus from the dead, and showed who was right after all. In the resurrection of Jesus the kingdom which he had declared to be near, so near that it was actually breaking through, in his word and works, is now inaugurated. For resurrection means precisely the coming of God's kingdom.

There is one passage in the New Testament which speaks of Jesus' resurrection in terms of his "vindication" or "justification," as in Isaiah 50. 7–11, namely 1 Tim. 3. 16 (vindicated in the Spirit). And in Rom. 4. 25 we read in what is now generally acknowledged to be an early credal formula, composed prior to Paul's use of it in his letter:

> who was put to death for our trespasses
> and raised *for our justification*.

It is tempting to conclude that as the early Church came to reflect on Jesus' death and resurrection and to interpret it in terms of Isaiah's suffering servant, it thought, as in Isaiah 50. 7–9, of Jesus' resurrection as *his* prior vindication (justification) before

13. See R. H. Fuller, *The Foundations of New Testament Christology* (London, 1965), pp. 153-4.

it went to speak of our vindication in him. In his resurrection Jesus is vindicated: he crosses over the line from this age into the kingdom of God, a transition which we too share through our identification with him in our baptism. True, Paul's doctrine of justification was a later theological elaboration, but, if we are right, it is elaborated out of the earlier application by the Church of the suffering servant songs to Jesus' passion and resurrection.

Wednesday in Holy Week:
Epistle (Hebrews 9. 16-28)[14]

This epistle was introduced at the Reformation (1549). Prior to that there was an Old Testament lesson, namely part of the last of the servant songs (Isaiah 52. 11—53. 7). This Old Testament lesson would be more fitting for Good Friday, and future revisers might consider (if they are going to make provision for these three days) using the first three Servant songs as Old Testament lessons on Monday, Tuesday, and Wednesday in Holy Week.

Our epistle from Hebrews would really be more suited for Maundy Thursday when we recall the institution of the euchar-ist, but the Pauline account of the institution now preempts that position. So apparently Heb. 9. 16–28 was put in the nearest place available, the day before. For this epistle recalls Moses' inauguration of the Old Covenant at Mount Sinai in Exodus 24. 6–8. The words of Moses, "This is the blood of the covenant" undoubtedly provide the model for St Mark's version of the cup-word of the eucharist: "This is *my* (as opposed to the Old Testament) blood-of-the-covenant." It is probably the liturgical tradition of his Church which has led the writer of Hebrews to return to this Exodus passage in order to prove (as he is concerned here to do) the necessity of Christ's death. His argument runs: "Christ's death inaugurated a covenant (the Greek word for "covenant" is the same as its word for "will" or testament). A will or testament does not come into force until the testator dies (vv. 15–17 the part omitted by the 1928 book, thus obscuring the context of the argument).[15] Then—returning to the primary

14 In 1928 BCP (but not Series I) the epistle was begun at v. 19.
15 These verses were restored in Series I.

91

meaning of covenant— the author observes that the first covenant likewise was inaugurated with "blood (i.e., deaths—the deaths of calves and goats). So too, he means to say, Christ's new covenant has to be inaugurated by blood. But the author gets so involved in the description of the scene in Exod. 24 (Heb. 9. 19–21) that he loses the original thread of his argument, and when he returns to Christ's sacrifice he makes the curious point (in line with his so-called Platonism, according to which every feature of the earthly cultus had its heavenly counterpart) that just as Moses cleansed the tent and all the vessels used in worship (v.21) so Christ cleansed the heavenly counterparts (v.23). One wonders what these counterparts are, and why they required cleansing if they belonged to the world of perfect reality! But apparently that point has not occurred to the author. What he wants to do from verse 23 on is to steer back from the Old Testament picture of Moses inaugurating the covenant to another Old Testament picture, that of the Levitical high priest entering the Holy Place annually to sprinkle the "things used in worship" there. So he can draw a second analogy. Not only is there an analogy between what Moses did on Sinai and what Christ did at Golgotha (both inaugurated a covenant by means of blood), but there is a further correspondence between the High Priest's annual entry into the Holy Place and Christ's entrance into heaven at his ascension For he "now [i.e., on the more probable interpretation, during the period between the ascension and the second coming] appears in the presence of God for us"; that is to say, the ground of our acceptance by God is the once-for-all death of Christ at Golgotha.

The most important verse in our epistle is verse 22b: "without the shedding of blood there is no forgiveness" (so RSV; AV is better: "remission": the Greek word means release from sin as a power holding human life in thrall). This poses the great problem with which Anselm wrestled, and which puzzled Harnack when he asked (with so many moderns): Why should not God have simply pronounced a word of forgiveness? Anselm's answer was that God's justice had to be satisfied before he could forgive, and Jesus, as the only perfectly innocent man, satisfied that claim of justice. But this answer is doubly at fault. Not only, as Gustav

Aulén showed, does this drive a wedge between the Father and the Son (the Father wanting justice and the Son stepping into the gap to fulfil it), but it makes the death of Jesus the precondition for, rather than the instrument of, atonement, forgiveness, and reconciliation. So Anselm really agrees with Abelard and Harnack in the end! God must *forgive* by just saying the word! What alternative rationale have we then to offer for the necessity of Christ's death for the atonement? Clearly any answer must do justice to the following facts:

1. It must, as Anselm rightly insisted, take with full seriousness the weight of man's sin and guilt.

2. It must preserve the historical happening of Golgotha, and not dissolve it into an illustration or declaration of a timeless truth.

3. It must preserve the continuity and simultaneity of action between the Father and the Son.

4. Therefore any doctrine of the atonement implies a prior doctrine of the Trinity and the incarnation.

5. Any answer must be shown to be not abstract theologizing, but must deal with the concrete historical realities of Jesus' passion on the one hand, and the concrete existential realities of human life on the other.

This is not the place to produce such a doctrine, for it requires much more space than we have at our disposal. But we would refer to our discussion of the word from the cross, "My God, my God, why hast thou forsaken me?" (above p. 85) and suggest that the answer is to be found in an interpretation of the death of Christ as God's own entering into complete involvement and identification with man in his state of alienation, and so actually overcoming it. We would claim that a doctrine of atonement along those lines fulfils the five requirements set forth above.

One of the most striking features of Holy Week is the reading of the Passions. The ancient Latin rite read the whole of St Matthew's Passion on Palm Sunday, St Luke's on Wednesday in Holy Week, and St John's on Good Friday. The Prayer Book, following the Reformers, divides Matthew into two, reading the first chapter at Morning Prayer and the second at the Communion. Then St Mark's Passion, which was not used anciently, is divided between Monday and Tuesday, and St Luke's between Wednesday and Thursday. And finally the Prayer Book treats St John's Passion on Good Friday as it had treated Matthew's on Palm Sunday, dividing it between Morning Prayer and the Liturgy.[16]

It is significant that the liturgy has to read the Passions *in toto*. They cannot be divided into small pericopes like the other liturgical gospels, for the Passion story has always existed— uniquely in the gospel material—as a continuous narrative from earliest times, before it was written down. Modern scholars in fact think that the Passions were the earliest parts of the Gospels to take shape, and it is a reasonable conjecture that they formed a kind of Christian "Passover haggada" from the first Christian celebration of the passover in the first year after the Crucifixion, *c*. A.D. 31. Whereas the Gospel pericopes are like separate snapshots, the Passions are more like a continuous film-strip. We say "like"—for they are not a contemporary record of what happened. There is of course a basic element of factual memory behind all four of our stories (really there are only three, (Mark, Luke and John) for Matthew is simply an embellishment of Mark).

We may outline the story as follows: Prompted by the provocative challenges of Jesus' entry into Jerusalem and his cleansing of the Temple, the Jewish authorities decided to get rid of him before the Passover. On the eve of the Passover Jesus cele-

---

16 Anciently the Passions were sung dramatically, three cantors taking the parts of the Christus, the minor parts and the narrator, while the choir sang the parts of the "turba" or crowd. It is out of this arrangement that the Passions of Johann Sebastian Bach were finally developed, Lutheran tradition before him having already enriched the narrative with congregational meditations and chorales.

brated a farewell meal with his disciples. At this meal he spoke to them of his impending departure and death, and of his certainty of restoration to fellowship with them in the consummated Kingdom of God. After the meal Jesus spent a vigil of solitary prayer in the Garden of Gethsemane. There he was betrayed, arrested, and then questioned by the Sanhedrin in order to establish a charge which could be brought before the occupying power. The real reason why they sought to get rid of him was doubtless a religious one, but only a political charge would compel the Romans to intervene. Probably Jesus remained silent when the High Priest asked him point blank, "Are you the Messiah?" (i.e., a claimant to the Jewish political throne). Alternatively, he may have replied "It's your word, not mine". Caiaphas took this as tantamount to tacit acceptance of the charge, and denounced Jesus before Pilate's court accordingly. (The charge "King of the Jews" is a translation into a Greek equivalent of the term Messiah so as to make it intelligible to Pilate). Pilate suspected that the charge was a false one and tried to release the prisoner, but yielded to the pressure of the authorities and of the crowd incited by them to release instead Barabbas, and to condemn Jesus to death by crucifixion. Meanwhile Jesus' disciples had forsaken him and fled, and one of them, Peter, had denied him. None of them was present at the trial scenes, but the ultimate plausibility of the foregoing summary is clinched by the title over the cross, which was displayed for all to see, "The King of the Jews". Jesus was undoubtedly crucified as a Messianic pretender. Some of the members of the Sanhedrin (such as Joseph of Arimathea and Nicodemus, if he is historical), who later joined the Christian movement, could vouch for the outline of what had happened when the disciples were not present.

Jesus was then brought from Pilate's official residence to the hill of Golgotha outside the city walls. The little episode of Simon of Cyrene who carried the cross seems to be vouched for by his two sons, Alexander and Rufus, probably members of the later Christian community where the tradition behind Mark took shape.

On arrival at the site of execution, Jesus may have been offered a drink of spiced wine to ease the pain, and the soldiers may have divided his garments among them, though it could be that both these features were suggested by Ps. 22. With stark simplicity all four Gospels state, "they crucified him"—they make no attempt to describe the physical or mental torture. Again, the mocking may have been suggested by Ps. 22, though it is not implausible. After a loud cry—variously articulated for theological motives in the "seven last words from the cross"—Jesus expires in the early afternoon, sooner than would have been expected. His demeanour to the end seems to have made a great impression on the centurion.

This much would have been recorded if a documentary of the passion had been made. For the rest, the Gospels have filled out the story with all sorts of theological movements.

The earliest Church preached that our Lord had died *"in accordance with the scriptures"* (1 Cor. 15. 3). In this way the Church convinced itself as well as proclaiming to its potential Jewish converts and adversaries the scandalous fact that he, who, they had come to believe, was indeed the Messiah of God, had been crucified. It was the will of God, the way he had planned his final act of redemption. The plan was foreshadowed in the sacred scriptures of Judaism itself. So the Church seized first upon Psalms 22 and 69 and later on Isa. 53, wove their language into the telling of the Passion Story, and to some degree allowed these passages to embroider the story with additional details. The words from the cross in particular become a repository for scripture fulfilments.

The Church proclaimed that *"Messiah* [Christ] died according to the scriptures". So the motif of the Messiahship or kingship of the Crucified—originally present indeed at the trial scenes and above all in the title on the cross—has received greater emphasis (e.g., in the soldiers' mockery and in the trial before Pilate).

Apologetic motives also came to play a part. For instance, Pilate's innocence is stressed at the expense of the Sanhedrin's guilt.

Symbolism plays a part—darkness covers the land at the Lord's dying. The Day of the Lord, said Amos, would be darkness, not light! The veil of the Temple is rent, betokening perhaps the breaking down of the middle wall of partition between God and man, or alternatively the entry of the Priest and Victim into the Holy Place (cf. Heb. 10. 19-20). To the ideal disciple is bequeathed the care of Jesus' Mother, who symbolizes the Church (John 19. 26f.). The earthquake and the rising of the saints after the death of Jesus (Matt. 27 51-53) proclaim that the End-time resurrection has been inaugurated by Jesus' death.

All these features show that we are meant to read the stories of the Passion not primarily as historical narratives but as proclamation of the Christian message of salvation through the death of Christ.

Each Evangelist, however, gives his own particular slant to the proclamation of that message.

Palm Sunday: St Matthew's Passion

Whereas Mark simply allows the Old Testament to colour the language in which he tells the Passion, Matthew calls special attention to scriptural fulfilment and quotes chapter and verse from the Old Testament as he does throughout his Gospel. This he does at Jesus' arrest (26. 54) and at the suicide of Judas (27. 9). Matthew emphasizes that it is God who delivers up the Son of man to death (the passive "will be delivered" is a reverential way of expressing an act of God) in 26. 2. The whole passion is an act of God himself, a mighty act of judgment and salvation, a point which is made again by the earthquake and by the resurrection of the saints at Jesus' death.

Repeatedly Matthew emphasizes Jesus' kingly majesty. He is the Son of God in his Passion. Twice Matthew adds "Son of God" to the mockery, first of the crowd (27. 40), then of the chief priest (27. 43). (It will be remembered how poignantly Johann Sebastian Bach underlines this—it is sung in unison at the end of the chorus by all eight parts.) To the soldiers' mocking of Jesus, Matthew adds a reed as a mock sceptre (27. 29).

Matthew stresses the innocence of Jesus. This innocence is not just a negative thing, but positive. It means positive obedience to the will of God. Pilate's wife sends a message to her husband

97

about Jesus' innocence (27. 19) and Pilate himself washes his hands of the whole business (27. 24). Jesus' enemies defiantly take all the guilt upon themselves: "His blood be on us and on our children" (27. 25).

Thus Matthew's portrait of the passion is a portrait of one who is at once King and yet humble, lowly, innocent, and obedient. Not despite of all this but precisely because of it all he is the majestic King. Truly the passion of Matthew goes very well with the Palm Sunday story—the paradoxical humility of the King.

Monday and Tuesday before Easter: St Mark's Passion

Since we do not possess Mark's source, it is not easy to detect alterations he has made to the story to bring out his own viewpoint. We have to judge it from the total impression it makes on us. Professor Christopher Evans has well characterized Mark's story: "Bare and unadorned, devoid of any literary artifice, and almost unbearably realistic, it moves rapidly from incident to incident. Once the action has begun it must go through to the end, which is, indeed, the bitter end. The sentences become shorter and shorter, the story staccato, like a train stuttering to a standstill".[17]

The next point that impresses us about St Mark's telling of the Passion is the complete passivity of Jesus. Hitherto, Jesus was supremely the active one—active in his proclamation, in calling the disciples to follow him, in driving out the demons, in his teaching in parables, in his resolute determination to go up to Jerusalem, in his triumphal entry and his cleansing of the temple, in his initiative over the arrangements for the last supper. Now, from Gethsemane on, he lets everything happen to him: his arrest, his refusal to defend himself at his examination and trial, in his being led to Golgotha, in his nailing to the gibbet, in his helpless cry, "My God, my God, why hast thou forsaken me", at the moment of his death. The Apostles' Creed says "suffered under Pontius Pilate", and the word "suffered" (*passus*) could

[17] C. F. Evans, "According to the Scriptures" in *Good Friday at St Margaret's* (London, 1957), p. 81.

be equally well translated "had things done to him". The whole passion narrative is in the passive mood. It is the passivity of complete obedience for which he had struggled in Gethsemane.

Coupled with Jesus' passivity is his utter loneliness. Judas betrayed him, the disciples forsake him and flee, Peter denies him, his friends stand afar off. His enemies are in remorseless league against him. The two thieves rail on him. Even the physical universe is blotted out in darkness.

What is the meaning of all this? It is, surely that Jesus engages in single-handed conflict with the powers of evil and darkness. In this conflict he is apparently passive, and yet it is precisely in this passivity that he is victorious. Once more St Paul provides the comment (and Mark was, in more ways than one, an excellent Paulinist) "He was crucified in weakness" (2 Cor. 13. 4)—yet paradoxically it is that weakness which is the power of God.

Wednesday and Thursday before Easter: St Luke's Passion

Luke certaintly had Mark's Passion narrative before him, but he has either edited it drastically and incorporated into it special traditions of his own, or else has chosen to use as the basis for his narrative another tradition altogether, contenting himself with carefully selected additions from Mark. As a result an entirely different picture emerges. Gone is the utter loneliness and the passivity of Mark's account. In Gethsemane, Luke's Jesus is strengthened by an angel from the Father. Luke's Jesus goes out to others in sympathy and evokes their sympathy in return. Luke's Jesus heals the priest's servant when the disciple cuts off his ear. He looks on Peter after the denial and wins Peter's penitence. The women of Jerusalem weep for him as he wends his way along the Via Dolorosa, and he calls out to them in sympathy, "Do not weep for me, but weep for yourselves and for your children" (Luke 23. 28). He prays (in most texts; some texts omit it probably because it was found incredible that Jesus should pray for the Jews), "Father, forgive them" (v. 34). Only one of the two thieves rails on him; the other repents, and receives from the dying Lord the promise, "Today you will be with me in

Paradise" (vv. 39-43). The crowds do not mock him. They watch him in silent sympathy, and return to the city beating their breasts. Instead of "My God, my God, why hast thou forsaken me,", Jesus dies with the Jewish child's bed-time prayer upon his lips, "Father, into thy hands I commit my spirit" (v. 46).

As has been fittingly remarked, Luke has transposed the passion from the key of tragedy to the key of pathos. Jesus is the first and great exemplar of Christian martyrdom. His example will soon be imitated by his first martyr, St Stephen (Acts 7). But Luke's Jesus is more than a martyr. He is the loving Saviour, whose suffering is the supreme expression of the sympathy and love he had shown throughout this gospel to the outcasts, the publicans and sinners, the women and the lost. The cross is the supreme revelation of the "tender love" of God towards mankind.

Good Friday: St John's Passion

Even if (as if becoming increasingly uncertain to scholars) John knew and used Mark's Gospel, it is clear that his Passion narrative is in no sense a re-editing of Mark, but rests upon an entirely different tradition. The main outline—the supper, the move to Gethsemane (not named), the arrest, the preliminary investigation before the high priest, Peter's denial, the trial before Pilate, the procession to Golgotha, the crucifixion and death—is the same. But the traits with which Mark emphasizes the loneliness and passivity of Jesus are gone. There is no cry of dereliction, no agonized prayer in the garden, no darkness over the earth. There is no sign, either, of the pathetic traits of Luke—no healing of Malchus' ear, no winsome look from Jesus to Peter after the denial, no weeping of the women or word of sympathy from Jesus, no "Father forgive them", no penitent thief. The nearest we come to pathos is the conversation between Jesus, his Mother, and the beloved disciple. But even this may be symbolic of the handing over of Mother Church to the Christian disciples, the new Israel.

St John's gospel is a highly theological document But John has put all his theology into the discourses during the ministry and at the Last Supper. When he comes to the Passion, there is very little theologizing. Only in the extended dialogue between

Jesus and Pilate, where Jesus is at pains to define his kingship in terms of witness to the "truth" (John 18. 33-8), do we have any echo of the theology of the earlier parts. All the rest of the Johannine theology—light, life, glory, etc.—is conspicuously lacking. John had expounded the theology of the Passion in the farewell discourses. Now he is content to let the facts as he has received them speak for themselves.

But the tradition he is using presents the facts in a way which underlines what the Evangelist had already said in the discourses about the Passion. John the Baptist had welcomed Jesus as the Lamb of God who takes away the sins of the world (John 1. 29). So Jesus' death occurs at the moment when the passover lambs are being slain (19. 30-31), not on the day after passover night, as in the synoptists. He dies with the cry, "It is accomplished" (19. 30, NEB)[18]—the true passover sacrifice has been offered. As with the passover lamb, not a bone of him is broken (v. 36).

More significant, perhaps is the way in which the story is told so as to bring out the force of Jesus' words earlier in the discourses, "I lay down my life, that I may take it again. No one takes it from me, but I lay it down of my own accord. I have power to lay it down, and I have power to take it again. This charge I have received from my Father" (John 10. 18). These words colour the whole of John's narration of the passion.

At the arrest it is Jesus, not the police, who takes the initiative. He voluntarily "comes forward" and sets the arrest in motion (18. 4). The police draw back and fall to the ground before his awesome majesty (v. 6). The disciples do not forsake Jesus and flee: he orders the police to let them go (v. 8). He stops Peter from trying to impede the course of events with the words: "Shall I not drink the cup which the Father has given me?" (v. 11). Willy-nilly, Jesus' adversaries bear witness to his kingship. Pilate says, "Here is your King" (19. 14). Some scholars have even suggested that "Behold the man", which Pilate says when he first brings Jesus before the people, means "Behold the Son of man" (19. 15). Later, when the Sanhedrin tries to bring pressure to bear on Pilate to tone down the inscription on the cross to read "This

[18] The RSV's retention of the A.V. (K.J.V.) "It is finished" is unpardonable. It is a cry of triumph (Latin Vulgate: *consummatum est*).

man said, I am the King of the Jews" (19. 21), Pilate stubbornly refuses, saying "What I have written, I have written". On the cross, Jesus arranges his will, bequeathes the disciples to the care of the Church, and the Church to the care of the disciples. All through, Jesus is in command of the situation, and at the very end he decides on the moment of his death: he does not expire, but gives up his spirit (the Holy Spirit?) (19. 30). All the way through, Jesus acts in sovereign majesty. He sets everything in motion, and decides at each moment what is to happen. He forces his enemies to testify to his majesty against their will.

This emphasis on the royal majesty of Jesus in his passion reminds us of Matthew's treatment (see above). But it is a majesty differently conceived. For Matthew it is a paradoxical majesty. For John it is an unqualified majesty. The cross *is* the lifting up of the Son of man, it *is* the hour when the Son of man is glorified.

Four Passion stories, four different presentations—the humble king; the lonely warrior wrestling in single combat (yet paradoxically utterly passive and weak) with the powers of darkness; the tender, loving Saviour, sympathizing with the lost and in return evoking love and sympathy; the majestic king in charge of the whole situation. Matthew, Mark, Luke, and John—they cannot be put together into a single sound-track film of the Passion. Rather, these are four proclamations of the cross from men of the Church who have come to know what the Passion means for this Church. The liturgy for Holy Week invites us to relive the passion of our Lord in four different ways.

7

THE TRIDUUM SACRUM

"Untranslatable into English, the Latin title of these last three days of Holy Week shows that together they form the most solemn period of the Christian year."[1]

They consist of the three days, Maundy Thursday, Good Friday, and the Easter Vigil. The present arrangements in the Book of Common Prayer and also the variety of ways in which these arrangements are carried out leave much to be desired. We shall have occasion to criticize both in the course of this chapter.

First, however, it is important to remember that the three holy days are the result of a development in which the unitary original paschal celebration (see above, pp. 11f.) has been split up into its component parts. This was done in the interest of historical commemoration. Thursday became the day for the commemoration of the Last Supper, Good Friday of the crucifixion, and Easter Day of the Resurrection. While we can now no longer go back behind these arrangements and recover the original practice of a fast and vigil, followed by the great paschal celebration in the night of Saturday–Sunday, we can at least hope to break away from a purely historical-commemorative treatment of these three days. We must learn to think of them as a single whole, in which the totality of our redemption is celebrated (not just historically commemorated) on each of the three days, but with a special emphasis on one aspect of one of its features on every day. Thus we shall celebrate Maundy Thursday as the total feast of our redemption, but with the special accent on the Last Supper as

[1] *A Directory of Ceremonial. Part II: The Liturgical Seasons* (Alcuin Club Tracts XIX), ed. G. B. Timms (London, 1965), p. 25.

the occasion on which the Lord's death was invested (in the institution narrative) with its saving significance. We shall celebrate Good Friday as the feast of our redemption with special emphasis on the cross, but remembering that we celebrate the cross precisely because of the resurrection which has revealed it to be what it is, namely, not a meaningless tragedy, but the act of God for us men and for our salvation. We shall celebrate the resurrection not as an isolated event in the biography of of Jesus, but as *transitus* of Jesus Christ from death to life and of our *transitus* in him.

MAUNDY THURSDAY

In Chapter 1 it was noted that the Jerusalem Church first established this day as a historical commemoration of the institution of the Lord's Supper. Later on, many other ceremonies and customs grew around the day and have left their traces on our present provisions. The penitents who had been placed under discipline on Ash Wednesday for the duration of Lent were restored to communion on this day. Today, too, the catechumens received a final exorcism in preparation for baptism. Oils were consecrated by the bishop for use in the services of the ensuing year (oil of exorcism, oil for confirmation, and oil for anointing the sick). Sovereigns washed the feet of beggars—a ceremony which still survives in Britain in a tenuous form: the Queen presents Maundy money to poor men and women to the number of her age. This last ceremony was based on our Lord's washing of the disciples' feet at the Last Supper, and the accompanying words command: "I have given you an example, that you also should do as I have done to you" (John 13. 15), and: "A new commandment I give unto you, that you love one another" (v. 34). The name "Maundy" comes from the Latin word for commandment, *mandatum*.

Most of these secondary associations have disappeared from the Anglican rites, except the commemoration of the Last Supper, this day's most primitive aspect which goes back to Bishop Cyril. It has survived in the epistle, St Paul's account of the Last Supper (1 Cor. 11. 23-34). Cranmer provided the second half of the Lucan passion as the gospel for this day, but recent Anglican revisions (not the English 1928 BCP) have gone further in Cyril's direction by restoring John 13. 1-15, the account of the footwashing, as the gospel, a change which is desirable in every way.

The late Dean of Chichester, A. S. Duncan-Jones, is said to have called Maundy Thursday the "Anglican Corpus Christi". The Latin feast of Corpus Christi, which falls on the Thursday after Trinity Sunday, was originally instituted in the thirteenth century in order to propagate the newly-defined dogma of Transubstantiation. All the Reformers were vehemently opposed to this doctrine, and so naturally they abolished this feast. Today, perhaps, we can see the Reformation controversy in a better perspective. What the Reformers were opposed to was the *popular* understanding of transubstantiation in a carnal materialistic sense. This gave rise to all sorts of abuses. There was the false notion that the priest made the bread and wine into Christ's body and blood and offered them to God as a propitiatory sacrifice additional to Calvary for the sins of the living and departed. Then there were the private masses, the cultus of the sacrament, etc. Today, however, we see that the dogma of transubstantiation was actually a serious attempt to safeguard the spiritual nature of the Real Presence in terms of medieval philosophy of substance (which meant not what we mean by "substance" today but the underlying spiritual reality of things) and "accidents".

Were the Reformers then right in abolishing Corpus Christi? Feasts celebrating dogmas were a late medieval innovation (cf. Trinity Sunday). The earlier idea was the celebration not of doctrines but of events or "mysteries" of our redemption. What the Reformers actually did in effect, however tentatively, was to restore the original Corpus Christi on Maundy Thursday. We celebrate on this day not so much a doctrine (though we would not deny the importance of the Real Presence as a doctrine) but the historical institution of a rite, of an action done by the Church. Many of the disputes over eucharistic doctrine, which have divided not only Catholics from Protestants but Protestants among themselves, could have been avoided had we realized that the Lord's command was, "Do this", rather than "Hold these doctrinal opinions about the meaning of what you are doing". The celebration of the "Anglican Corpus Christi" on Maundy Thursday had therefore important ecumenical consequences.

Another argument in favour of celebrating Corpus Christi on Maundy Thursday is that it sets the celebration of the institution of the Lord's Supper in closest connection with the redemptive events or mysteries which the Supper itself celebrates and makes present in their effects—the passion and resurrection of the Saviour. The sacraments are not things in themselves, but actions "rivetted" (the word was Hoskyns') to the redemptive events.

Outside the Church of England these tentative efforts of the Reformers have been taken further. The Canadian Prayer Book of 1959 (p. 169) has adopted for Maundy Thursday the collect which Thomas Aquinas composed for Corpus Christi; and which now appears in *Alternative Services First Series* for any occasion of thanksgiving for the institution of Holy Communion:

> O Lord, who in a wonderful Sacrament hast left us a memorial of thy passion: Grant us so to reverence the holy mysteries of thy Body and Blood, that we may ever know within ourselves the fruit of thy redemption; who livest etc.

The American Prayer Book (p. 152) has a modern composition for its collect, but of similar import to the more ancient collect of the Canadian book. It runs as follows:

> Almighty God, whose dear Son, on the night before he suffered, did institute the Sacrament of his Body and Blood; Mercifully grant that we may thankfully receive the same in remembrance of him, who in these holy mysteries giveth us a pledge of life eternal . . ..

This collect makes the additional and valuable point that the proper way to give thanks for the institution of the Sacrament is precisely to *receive* it (rather than to have extra-liturgical devotions like Benediction). Also, the assertion that in these holy mysteries we receive a "pledge of life eternal" strikes the eschatological note so often lacking in our modern western sacramental theology, but very prominent in the New Testament. Jesus had given the Supper to his disciples as a foretaste of the banquet of the kingdom of God (Mark 14. 25, Luke 22. 15-18). St Paul insisted that we celebrate the eucharist "until he comes" (1 Cor. 11. 26). And the eucharistic discourse in John 6 has the constant refrain that those who eat the flesh and drink the blood of the Son of man will be "raised up at the last day".

Anglican calendars customarily follow the tradition derived originally from the bishop's blessing of the oils, and prescribe the use of Festal white as the liturgical colour for the Lord's Supper (only). Despite its quite different origin, this usage has a great psychological value. The Maundy Lord's Supper stands out in its highly festal character from the other services of Holy Week:

> This is the hour of banquet and of song;
> This is the heavenly table spread for me;
> Here let me feast, and feasting, still prolong
> The brief, bright hour of fellowship with thee.
>
> (*Hymnal 1940*, P.E.C.U.S.A. no. 206)

How unfitting though, is the continuation of the Lucan passion in that setting. It is to be hoped that all future Anglican revisions will complete the Lucan passion on Wednesday of Holy Week, and restore John 13 for the gospel of Maundy Thursday.

The Maundy Thursday eucharist is indeed a "brief, bright hour" before we plunge into the darkness of Good Friday. On this day, above all other days of the year, it is most desirable that the Lord's Supper be celebrated in the evening. Fortunately, Rome's recent reforms have now made this entirely respectable, and most Episcopal churches in the U.S.A. have restored it. Although an evening celebration on Maundy Thursday is growing in popularity in all schools of church manship, the Church of England has far to go before it will cease to be fair to say that it is lagging somewhat behind the American Episcopalians, and the new edition of Percy Dearmer's *Parson's Handbook* is excessively antiquarian on this point.[2]

---

[2] P. Dearmer, *The Parson's Handbook*. Revised by C. E. Pocknee (London 1965), p. 103.

GOOD FRIDAY

Originally, Good Friday was an "a-liturgical" day, i.e., a day on which there was no public service of any kind. The faithful were supposed to spend the day in silent vigil and fast. Only on the Saturday evening was this silence broken with the vigil service. The Church fasted on the day on which the bridegroom was taken away (Mark 2. 20).

Traces of the original a-liturgical character still remain in various places. In the Latin rite, this has always been a day when the eucharist was not consecrated. Communion in the Roman Church on this day is administered from the reserved sacrament, consecrated on Maundy Thursday. Until Rome's recent reforms only the priest received communion on this day. But recently the communion of the people from the reserved sacrament has been restored (this service is known as the Mass of the Pre-sanctified, i.e., a Mass in which the elements have been consecrated beforehand). Post-Reformation Anglican practice (like the Lutheran), however, for the first time in history introduced the full celebration of the Holy Communion on this day, with a consecration of the elements. In the middle of the last century Anglicans widely returned to the much earlier practice of having only antecommunion (this is even earlier than general communion from the reserved sacrament), the first part only of the liturgy, the service of the word. Just recently, however, there has been a reaction in some circles in favour of having a full celebration, as in old-fashioned Anglican, and in normal Lutheran practice.[3] It seems likely that in years to come (since there is a desire for something more satisfying than the somewhat jejune provision of antecommunion, and since also the practice of general communion from the reserved sacrament would be somewhat exotic for most Anglicans), that Anglican practice will

[3] For arguments in favour of this see John T. Martin, *Christ our Passover* (Studies in Ministry and Worship No. 4), (London, 1958), pp. 32-34; J. Gordon Davies, *Holy Week: A Short History* (Ecumenical Studies in Worship No. 11), (London and Richmond, Va., 1963), p. 69; C. P. M. Jones (ed.) *A Manual for Holy Week* (London, 1967) v. index s.v. "Good Friday, celebration of Eucharist on".

increasingly return to what it was before 1850, and what it still is in Lutheranism today.

The different accentuation and association of the three days of the Triduum could be brought out by celebrating the eucharist at different times and in a different way each day. The Maundy Thursday eucharist would come appropriately at the time of the Last Supper, "the night that he was betrayed", i.e., after sundown. It is white and festal. The Good Friday eucharist would come most appropriately during the three hours, between 12 noon and 3 p.m. on Good Friday, when the Saviour hung on the cross and where there was darkness over the earth (though practical reasons, especially in the U.S.A. and parts of England where people have to work, may make it necessary to have it later in the afternoon). The sanctuary would be stripped bare, but the liturgical colour used is the subdued red of passiontide.[4] The Easter celebration would come in the very early morning, either "while it was still dark" (John 20. 1), or "very early . . . when the sun had risen" (Mark 16. 2).

GOOD FRIDAY: THE COLLECTS

The Latin provisions for Good Friday which provided the main source for the Book of Common Prayer have a number of primitive features. One of these is the lack of any collect (collects came into the Western liturgy only in the mid fifth-century). The Reformers clearly could not tolerate these anomalous features, despite their primitive character, and made provisions for Good Friday which would make it like any other day. Hence our three collects.

Good Friday: Collect 1

The first collect was taken from the Latin post-communion collect of Wednesday in Holy Week, and ultimately from the Gregorian Sacramentary. Its words "given up into the hands of wicked men" are indeed more suitable for Wednesday, the traditional day of

[4] "It is to be desired that red should replace the black on Good Friday. The Church cannot be in mourning for her Saviour, but she should celebrate him as a King who has gained victory through his blood outpoured on the cross", Max Thurian. *The Eucharistic Memorial, Part I*, The Old Testament, Tr. J. G. Davies. (Ecumenical Studies in Worship No. 7), (London and Richmond, Va. 1960-61, p. 67.

the Lord's betrayal. The petition does not seem very concrete: "graciously to behold". But it must mean "look with the eyes of favour", "extend thy grace to", and rests upon the fact that the cross is the supreme revelation and actualization of the grace of God. "Family" is of course the household of the Church. Against the term "wicked" men one might protest that the men who executed Jesus were not particularly wicked. In fact, the real point about them is precisely that they were ordinary people. The wicked referred to are of course the Romans into whose hands Jesus was "given up". Pilate did at least try to get Jesus released, and that he should have yielded to pressure, was only too human, and not particularly wicked. The soldiers were doubtless no better and no worse than the soldiers or police of any other country—capable of indulging in acts of brutality on helpless victims just for the fun of it. The Latin word (*nocentium*) suggests precisely this brutality, for it means "harmful" men.

Good Friday: Collects 2 and 3

Much more distinctive are the second and third collects. One of the most striking features of the unusual and very primitive Latin rite of Good Friday was the series of intercessions with which the service of the Word closed. These intercessions go back to the earliest days of Christianity and even beyond it to the Jewish synagogue, both in the place in which they occur (right at the end of the service of the word) and in their pattern. We in the modern Church, who are used to three conventional forms of intercession, the collect, the priestly monologue, and the litany, would do well to recover this ancient type of intercession. This is its pattern, still discernible in the Roman Mass:

First, the priest announces a bidding or subject for prayer. He then says, "Let us pray". The deacon issues the command, "Let us kneel". The people then kneel in silent prayer. Then the sub-deacon issues the command, 'Arise", and the people do so. Gregory Dix has commented aptly on this very ancient pattern of intercession:

All christendom was then [in the early fourth century] still at one on the way in which the public intercession should be offered: by a corporate act involving the whole church, in which nevertheless each order—laity, deacon, and officiant (bishop or presbyter)—must actively discharge its own separate and distinctive function within the fulfilment of the "priestly" activity of the whole Body of Christ. It offers to God not only itself in its organic unity, but all the world with its sorrows and its busy God-given natural life and its needs (op. cit., p. 45).

Dix then goes on to contrast this with the modern forms of public intercession, in which the clergy have taken over the whole of the praying, and reduced the laity to a single Amen. In some Protestant traditions they do not even join in this! As a result, says Dix, the laity imagine that real prayer, including intercessory prayer, is done in solitude, instead of private prayer being an extension of liturgical prayer. All this, he continues, is a product of the clericalism of the middle ages, which the Reformers unfortunately failed to abolish. Luther asserted, quite rightly, the doctrine of the priesthood of all believers, but by and large the believers have not been given much opportunity to exercise this priesthood corporately in the liturgy, which remains as clerically dominated as before.

While, unfortunately, Cranmer abolished this ancient form of intercession which survived on Good Friday, he did take up some of the subject matter of the nine intercessory prayers of the Latin rite and fashioned it into a second and third collect for Good Friday.

The Latin intercession on which our second collect was based was the summary of the private prayer of the congregation in response to the bidding, "Let us also pray for all Bishops, Priests, Deacons, Subdeacons, Acolytes, Exorcists, Lectors, Doorkeepers, Confessors, Virgins, Widows, and for all the holy people of God". The Latin collect went on to pray for all the "orders" of the Church. Cranmer's composition prays in merely general terms for all "estates" of men in the church, but in a way thoroughly characteristic of Reformation thought (the break-down of the unwarranted division between sacred and secular), and explicitly recognizes that *every* member (not only those in holy orders) has a "vocation and ministry".

111

Good Friday: The Third Collect

The 1662 Prayer Book includes the petition: "Have mercy upon all Jews, Turks, Infidels, and Hereticks"; all revisions have toned this down. This was based on the seventh bidding and its collect in the Latin rite which referred to the "faithless Jews". Pope John XXIII, it will be recalled, personally changed this somewhat offensive reference. Yet it is wholly appropriate that on this day we should pray for all who do not know the love of God in Christ crucified, when he himself prayed, "Father, forgive them; for they know not what they do" (Luke 23. 24). It is also wholly appropriate that intercession should figure so largely in today's liturgy. For the cross is the supreme act of intercession, and all intercession is the Church's joining with the intercession of the crucified. This intercession which he offered on the cross is now continued by the great High Priest, on the ground of his once-for-all sacrifice on the cross, where he now ever liveth to make intercession for us (Heb. 7. 25), and where he for ever appears in the presence of God on our behalf (Heb. 9. 24). When we offer intercession, we do so as members of his body on earth, joined with the Head and High Priest in the priesthood of the body. On earth we know not how to pray as we ought, but the Spirit helps us in our weakness with sighs too deep for words (Rom. 8. 26), taking our weak and feeble prayers, transforming them and joining them the great intercession of our heavenly High Priest.

It is surely to be regretted that, although the Prayer Book has retained something of this intercessory feature in its collects, it nevertheless has not preserved the full and ancient provisions of the Latin rite. True, we can do something more in this direction, even within the terms of our present provisions. For we still have a Bidding Prayer (revised in the overseas Churches of the Anglican Communion), each petition of which could be followed by silence and by a collect in the ancient manner. It would come appropriately in the traditional position at the end of the service of the Word, in the place where the Prayer for the Church normally comes. The Prayer for the Whole State of Christ's Church could then be omitted.

Good Friday: The Epistle (Heb. 10. 1-25)

The Latin rite again followed the primitive use in having no epistle but two Old Testament lessons, Hosea's prophecy of the resurrection (Hos. 6. 1-6), which some scholars think is the passage which the New Testament writers had in mind when they proclaimed that Christ was raised the third day in *accordance with the scriptures* (1 Cor. 15. 3) and Exod. 12. 1-11, the institution of the Passover. Both of these lessons belonged originally to the unitary Paschal feast, and have wandered somewhat inappropriately to the now separated commemoration of the crucifixion. It is to be hoped that they will not be forgotten in any Anglican restoration of the ancient vigil service, where they would properly belong. The compilers of the BCP clearly felt the unsuitability of these lessons for Good Friday, and in accordance with their general desire to remove the apparent anomalies of the day, provided an epistle from Hebrews. For an observation on the contribution of this passage to an understanding of the Lord's death as a sacrifice see above, pp. 70f.

For comment on the gospel (the Passion according to St John), see above, pp. 100-102.

EASTER EVEN
A PECULIARLY ANGLICAN INTERLUDE

Originally the Saturday morning in Holy Week was another a-liturgical period like Good Friday, being part of the silent fast preceding the vigil service. In the middle ages the vigil service, together with many additional ceremonies which had grown up around it such as the kindling of the new fire, the lighting of the paschal candle, the blessing of the font and the litany of the saints, and the ensuing first Mass of Easter, was shifted further and further back until eventually the whole complex came to be celebrated on Saturday morning. This was incongruous, both liturgically in view of the many references in the text of the liturgy to "this holy night", and also historically in view of the fact that the Lord was still in the tomb on the Saturday morning.

It should be a matter of ecumenical gratification that the Roman Church has recently moved this service back to the place where it properly belongs, namely to a late hour on Saturday night. Thus once more the great Easter eucharist may be celebrated after midnight. The result at Rome presumably is to leave the morning of Holy Saturday an a-liturgical period as it was originally, with no propers of its own.

The English reformers solved the problem somewhat differently, and not altogether happily. They abolished lock, stock, and barrel all the Easter ceremonies (the new fire, paschal candle, the blessing of the font) including the most primitive and evangelical feature of all, the reading of the prophecies, which came from the old vigil service, as well as the litany of the saints. Thus they threw away the good with the bad, including by a strange irony what had been the original Easter eucharist itself! And instead of keeping Holy Saturday a-liturgical they put in its place a new series of propers (epistle and gospel) featuring the Lord's entombment. This was an Anglican invention and an Anglican peculiarity. Yet perhaps it was not quite without value, for it takes up the clause, "and was buried" in the creed which otherwise receives little or no recognition in the liturgical year (except perhaps at Evening Prayer on Good Friday).

Easter Even: The Collect

The collect comes not from Cranmer's pen, but from the revisers of 1662 following the Scottish Prayer Book of 1637. Till then there was no proper collect for this day, and the Palm Sunday collect was simply repeated as throughout the week.

The wording of this collect takes up St Paul's exposition of baptism in Rom. 6. 3ff. as the participation of the faithful in the death and resurrection of Christ. It thus had the merit of keeping alive since the seventeenth century the memory of Easter Even as the great day for baptisms. This memory had not been forgotten altogether at the time of the Reformation, for a rubric at the beginning of the baptismal service read:

It appeareth by ancient writers, that the Sacrament of Baptism in the old time was not commonly ministered, but at two times in the year, at Easter and Whitsuntide, at which times it was openly ministered in the presence of all the congregation.

(*First Prayer Book of Edward VI*, 1549, spelling modernized)

Easter Even: The Epistle (1. Pet. 3. 17-22)

This is a rather confused passage which combines the thought of the flood as a type of baptism with Christ's preaching to the spirits in prison. Obviously it was thought that this mythological "event" occurred between the burial and resurrection. The more probable exegesis is that the author of 1 Peter links the preaching with Christ's triumph at his Ascension over the powers of evil.

Easter Even: The Gospel (Matt. 27. 57-66)

This is the story of the burial of Jesus through the good offices of Joseph of Arimathea and the subsequent sealing of the tomb and setting of the watch. The latter two points are apologetic additions by Matthew to his Marcan source. They were intended as a counterblast to the Jewish slander that the disciples stole the body of their Master and staged the resurrection.

The earliest credal formula in the New Testament contained a reference to the burial of Jesus (1 Cor. 15. 4, "that he was buried"). In that formula it serves the function of underlining the reality of the death of Jesus as the parallel phrase "he appeared" in v. 5 underlines the reality of the resurrection. The story of the burial as we find it in Mark clearly goes back to early Jerusalem tradition, as the name of Joseph of Arimathea and the testimony of the women indicates. As a real man, Jesus experiences the finality of death. Apart from an unprecedented miracle of God—the miracle of resurrection—that is the end, for Jesus as for every man.

No provision is made for this in the BCP. Yet this was the greatest service of the whole Christian year, as well as the climax of Lent. It was to this service that the penitential exercises of Ash Wednesday, the catechumenal instruction of Lent I-III, the refreshment of Mid-Lent, the solemnities of Passiontide and Holy Week should all have been tending, the great paschal vigil and eucharist. For it is not enough after all this simply to plunge into Easter on Sunday morning. If we are to recover the rhythm of biblical, evangelical, primitive Christianity, our liturgical observance of Easter must somehow include the most vital experience which the most ancient liturgical provisions afforded. This is the *transitus*, the passing over from passion to resurrection, from death to life, from sin to righteousness, from bondage to freedom, from darkness to light. This is the fulfillment of the Passover of the old covenant, the night on which the children of Israel passed out of the bondage of Egypt into freedom. Our present liturgical provisions, taking Holy Week, Good Friday, and Easter Day together, do provide the two sides of the *transitus*. There is passion, and there is resurrection. There is death, and there is life. There is darkness, and there is light. But the transition between them, the "passover" itself, is lacking. This is more than a loss of drama. It is more than a lack of the experience of the transition. To some extent those who have been through Holy Week and Good Friday have some sense of this when they come to church on Easter morning. They are aware of the contrast between the service of Good Friday, and the service on Easter Day. But there are many who come to church only on Easter Day, and who have missed Holy Week and Good Friday completely. They get resurrection without passion, life without death, righteousness without awareness of sin, freedom without awareness of the bondage from which they have been delivered, light without the darkness. This is cheap grace, which ignores the cost of discipleship. The fullness of the gospel demands the recovery of both sides of the transition, and it would seem that the only way of doing so would be to restore something like the old vigil service, held in the night of Easter Even–Easter Day.

THE EASTER VIGIL SERVICE AND
THE PASCHAL EUCHARIST

We have referred a number of times to the desirability of restoring the so-called Vigil service of Easter Eve. But it is important that we should be quite clear what we are doing. The name "Vigil service" is somewhat misleading when applied to the *whole* service, for it suggests a service which is only preparatory to the proper occasion. It gives the impression that we are proposing an additional service which will prepare for the Easter morning services which we already have, and that this morning service will still remain intact as the proper celebration of Easter. This mode of thinking—although it is often expressed or subconsciously assumed, and even seems to underlie some of the pronouncements of various liturgical commissions—is the reverse of the truth. The Easter Day service (even the early service of the American and other revisions which have put back the first Easter Mass of the 1549 Book) of the Prayer Book belongs not to the Paschal Eucharist but rather to the series of services during Easter week itself. The difference is clear. The so-called Vigil service, as we have noticed frequently, is the *transitus*, the Christ's passage (and the passage of his people through baptism) from death to life, from darkness to light, from sorrow to joy, etc. During the Octave of Easter we now celebrate the Easter events by commemorating them historically—the empty tomb and the appearances, while for the rest of *Pentecoste* or great fifty days we celebrate the new life which we have in Christ.

Originally the Easter Vigil was conducted like this. The short 24–48 hour pre-Easter fast was observed privately until sometime between 6 p.m. on Saturday and 3 a.m. on Sunday. Then two simultaneous but separate assemblies were held, Easter baptisms in the baptistry, and the other in the main assembly room for the reading of an Old Testament series of prophecies as in other vigil services by the faithful. Then the two congregations joined together for the celebration of the paschal eucharist, at which the newly initiated received Holy Communion for the first time.

With the disuse of adult baptism as a normal practice, the

separate baptismal assembly was abandoned, and its place was eventually taken by the somewhat meaningless blessing of the font after the reading of the prophecies. Also, the somewhat later (c. 700) picturesque ceremonies of the blessing of the new fire and the lighting of the paschal candle, and from it all the lights in the darkened church. The former of these is probably of pagan origin and its theological significance uncertain. The latter may be ultimately of Jewish origin, and have passed into Christian usage as a regular evening ceremony, for which the hymn *Phos Hilaron*[5] was originally composed. The blessing of the candle is accompanied by the thrilling Easter proclamation called the *Exultet*. Another later addition to the Vigil service was the litany sung in procession to and from the font. The blessing of the font is an attenuated survival from the ancient baptismal rite.

How much of these later accretions shall we want to preserve, restore, or modify?

The lighting of the paschal candle is becoming increasingly popular, and has official sanction in the *Book of Offices* of PECUSA.[6] The blessing of the fire with its pagan origin and uncertain Christian significance could well be dropped. But the Easter proclamation which accompanies the lighting is the feature we shall want to preserve or restore more than anything else (though as is generally agreed the text needs considerable pruning). For here is stated the threefold mystery which is celebrated this night:

> This is the night, wherein thou didst lead forth our (*sic*) fathers, the children of Israel, out of Egypt, making them pass over the Red Sea on dry land. This is the night, wherein all who believe in Christ are delivered from the shadow of death, and are renewed unto grace and made partakers of everlasting life. This is

[5] E. H. 269. For several years we used this hymn at Seabury-Western Theological Seminary after the lighting of the paschal candle, and it is interesting to find the same custom in the Diocese of Southwark. See G. Hudson in C. P. M. Jones, op. cit., p. 84.

[6] New York, 1960—but with a serious blunder: the ceremony *precedes* Evening Prayer (rubric, p. 101). The latter service belongs not to Easter Day, but to the Eve, whose collect it should have (a fact to which Church Calendars in the U.S.A. have only recently awoken!). For the right order see *A Directory of Ceremonial II* (Alcuin Tracts 19) (London, 1965), p. 81.

the night wherein Christ loosed the bonds of hell, and from the grave did rise again victorious over sin.[7]

It might be an improvement to reverse the order here so that the three *transitûs* come in their proper historical and theological order: the exodus, the death-resurrection of Christ, and the baptisms of Christian believers.

It is most desirable that the blessing of the paschal candle should be moved from its traditional position to a place after the prophecies and before the baptism.[8] Thus rearranged, the service will have a remarkable coherence. First, we recall the Old Testament types and prophecies of the Christian *transitus*, next we celebrate the threefold *transitus* itself (with the *transitus* of the Messiah himself in the centre of our celebration), then we proceed with the sacrament of initiation (or at very least the renewal of baptismal vows) in which our *transitus* is accomplished on the basis of Christ's. It might present a problem to read the prophecies in the darkened church, but they seem to manage it in the Diocese of Southwark.[9]

Until the revision of 1956, the Latin rite contained twelve prophecies. These have now been reduced to four, viz.:

1. The Creation story (Gen. 1).
2. The Crossing of the Read Sea (Exod. 14)
3. The Song of the Vineyard (Isa. 5)
4. The Old Covenant (Deut. 23)

Mr J. P. Martin has put forward the sensible suggestion that different lessons could be chosen from the provisions of ancient liturgies for different years,[10] and lists for that purpose a pool of eighteen such lessons which have been used in the past.[11] However, Exod. 14 should be invariable.

While most recent Anglican proposals have advocated the renewal of baptismal vows to follow after the prophecies, it must

[7] Text from the *Book of Offices* (p. 101).
[8] Cf. C. P. M. Jones (ed.), op. cit., pp. 73, 75 and 83. I am glad to find that these authorities feel what I have long felt, but had never seen expressed.
[9] ibid., p. 83.
[10] John P. Martin, op. cit., p. 44.
[11] ibid., p. 44, n. 1.

be remembered that anciently the full rites of Christian initiation (baptism and "confirmation") took place at this time. It is quite likely that, without repudiating infant baptism, we shall for a number of reasons (the secularization of modern society, our readiness to review our own tradition in the light of the ecumenical witness of the Baptists, and the desire to recover unity by returning to primitive wholeness) move gradually towards the administration of adult initiation (following, in the case of Christian families, the enrolment of children as catechumens) as the regular procedure. Therefore, we ought to place the full initiation rite here (and it should be of the pattern suggested by the Liturgical Commission of the Church of England[12]), even if the service in its fullness is rarely performed. A renewal of the baptismal vows by those already baptized would naturally accompany this, as suggested by the Reformation rubric, which argues for the administration of baptism (of infants) in the presence of the congregation "Because . . . every man present may be reminded of his profession to God in his baptism". This is a valuable suggestion, and any attempt to revive separate baptistries and hidden baptisms such as is advocated in some quarters on the ground that this was the use of the primitive church should be firmly rejected as sheer antiquarianism. Only in default of an actual baptism is it necessary to provide a special renewal of baptismal vows for the already baptized. In either case this represents for the faithful the climax of their Lenten devotions, and the goal for which they have been striving since Ash Wednesday.

The great Easter Eucharist, the chief service in the Church year (at present not in our Prayer Books!) now follows. Since we have already had a service of the Word, there is no reason why this service should not begin at the offertory and proceed at once to the Eucharistic prayer, the breaking of bread and the Communion. This would solve a major problem to which too little attention has been given. We refer to the liturgical gospel for this Eucharist. Recalling our oft-repeated statement that the

[12] See their report presented with the Second Series services of Baptism and Confirmation (S.P.C.K. 1967), and the services themselves as authorized in 1968.

Vigil service celebrated the triple *transitus* (Israel, Christ, and the Baptized), with Christ's own *transitus* in the centre; and recalling also the fact that the gospels of Easter week (of which our present Easter Day provisions form a part) focus not upon the resurrection itself, but on the events upon which the resurrection faith is based, namely, the empty tomb and the appearances, we are left wondering where an appropriate Easter gospel is to be found. For, as is well known, the gospels and the New Testament never narrate the resurrection itself, i.e., the act of God in raising Jesus from the dead. Indeed, it cannot be related at all, for it is not strictly speaking (in the sense of a humanly observed and verifiable event) an historical event at all, but a confession of faith arising from the revelation contained in the appearances. We know it only by the apostolic testimony, "Christ is risen". We shall, therefore, seek in vain for a really adequate gospel. About the worst we could do would be to retain the Johannine or Marcan stories of the empty tomb[13] which are in present use for the Easter Day services. For despite the attraction Professor Altizer feels for the empty tomb as the quintessential end of Jesus' story, this is not what the Church or the New Testament proclaims, least of all on Easter Day. If it is felt essential to have a gospel at this Eucharist, perhaps the best choice would be the Matthean version of the empty tomb (Matt. 28. 1-7). This was anciently the gospel at the midnight service in the Latin rite,[14] as it still is in the Eastern Orthodox Church. The justification for this restoration would be that the Matthean pericope is the only attempt in the New Testament to approach (though with a considerable hesitation which has frequently been contrasted with the apocryphal *Gospel of Peter*) anything like a description of the actual resurrection, viz., the earthquake, the descent of the angel, and the opening of the grave. But these features are, of course, late in the gospel tradition and are clearly legendary in character. The Easter proclamation should be sufficient.

[13] The Johannine story is the sole provision of English 1662 and 1928. The Marcan gospel has been revived from 1549 in some Anglican revisions for a "first" celebration.

[14] Whence it wandered with the Vigil service to early Saturday morning: it is now restored to the midnight service.

A liturgical sermon is hardly necessary on this occasion. As the present writer contended some years ago,[15] the function of the liturgical sermon understood at its deepest theological level is to recall (by means of the gospel) the basic events of the kerygma into which the faithful were baptized so that the Church can celebrate these events anew in the eucharist and partake anew in their benefits. Since all this is done in the service (especially where the full rite of initiation is administered in its integrity), there is no need for a sermon here. The whole liturgy itself is an adequate Easter Sermon, summed up in the Easter proclamation: *Christos aneste*, Christ is risen!

[15] R. H. Fuller, *What is Liturgical Preaching?* (London, 1957), p. 12.

APPENDIX

THE PRAYER BOOK EASTER DAY

It is little short of tragic that the "most important service of the whole year"[1] the Easter Vigil, has disappeared, practically without trace, from the present provisions of the Book of Common Prayer. With it, as we saw in the final chapter has gone the thrilling experience of the *transitus*. The only distinct survival of the old vigil service that we have in the 1662 book is the epistle (Col. 3. 1-7).[2]

The collect of Easter Day is derived from a second Mass celebrated in the Latin rite on Easter Day itself after the vigil, which came to be thought of as the real service for the day when the vigil service was shifted back to the morning of Easter Even. The gospel of the 1662 service, the Johannine account of the empty tomb, again does not in the Latin rite belong to Easter Day at all, but to the Saturday after Easter. These facts are not just of antiquarian interest, but are important for understanding our present (1662) Easter Day propers. This service, as it now stands belongs not to the transition from Lent to Easter, but rather to the services of the *Pentecoste*—the Great Fifty Days of the Easter season. This season has quite a different rationale from the *transitus* of the Easter Vigil. "These fifty days were held as

[1] Quoted by W. K. Lowther Clarke and Charles Harris, op. cit. p. 393f. from J. W. Tyrer, *Historical Survey of Holy Week* (Alcuin Club, London 1932), p. 147.

[2] Originally the epistle was shorter (Col. 1. 1-4). 1549 BCP lengthened it; American 1928 reverted to the shorter form. It is a precious link with the old vigil service for it speaks of the faithful as risen with Christ in their baptism, and the need to implement this in life.

123

one long period of thankfulness for the fact of the Resurrection and the experience of the Resurrection life."[3]

During this period, part of the focus of interest is on the historical events which gave rise to the Easter faith, namely the empty tomb and the post-resurrection appearances. Other lessons of this kind which survive in the Prayer Book provisions are the appearance stories on Easter Monday (the Emmaus story from Luke 24), on Easter Tuesday (the Lucan version of the appearance to the Eleven), and Low Sunday (the Johannine version of the appearance to the Eleven).

The 1549 Prayer Book provided a collect, epistle, and gospel for a "second Communion" on Easter Day. The collect was our present collect for Easter 1 (in 1549 it did also duty for Easter 1); the epistle 1 Cor. 5. 6-8 (which in the Latin rite is the epistle for the second Easter Mass corresponding to 1662 the service for Easter Day) and the gospel the Marcan version of the empty tomb (Mark 16. 1-8). The American BCP has restored these provisions with the exception of the collect, which is from another ancient source.[4]

It is questionable whether the statement[5] that this first 1549 Mass "corresponds to the vigiliary Mass" is correct. The place of its propers in the Latin rite does not bear this out. As far as the gospel is concerned, it belongs to the Eastertide series (the events which created the Easter faith) rather than to the *transitus*.

In this book we have deliberately refrained from presenting the type of treatment on the Easter Day propers which we have given for those of Lent, since with the exception of the epistle these provisions belong integrally to Eastertide (*Pentecosté*) rather than, as the old vigil service did, to Lent itself.

[3] H. de Candole, in *The Calendar and Lectionary*, ed. Ronald C. D. Jasper (London, 1967) p. 4. This work arrived too late to be used in the body of this work.

[4] It is immediately derived from the little service "before Mattins" in 1549, a survival of the Sarum Easter procession. The ultimate source of this collect is the Gregorian sacramentary. In England it will be found in the 1928 book as an additional collect for Easter week.

[5] K. D. Mackenzie in W. K. Lowther Clarke and C. Harris, op. cit., p. 393.